(Continued from front flap)

as attempted to chart a "third course"
...n capitalism and bureaucratic
...munism—a socialist humanism with-
bias or privilege, without arbitrariness
illegality, and without a Party mo-
oly of power. Though he remains a
terialist, a Marxist, and a socialist, he
s for a flexible policy of peaceful,
lutionary social change in accord with
facts of a changing political and
nomic world.

ANATOMY OF A MORAL is more than a
gle man's intellectual rebellion against
mmunist theory and practice. It is, in
dition, the ideological journey which
ny Communist intellectuals and lead-
have taken since the death of Stalin,
d a pathway which many more will
e as they grow increasingly disen-
anted by the gap between Communist
omises and fulfillments. And it is pre-
sely in this metamorphosis that there
s a great hope both for the West and
r the peoples of the Communist world.

anatomy
of a
moral

anatomy
of a
moral

the political essays of

MILOVAN
DJILAS

Edited by Abraham Rothberg

With an Introduction by Paul Willen

FREDERICK A. PRAEGER, *Publishers*

NEW YORK

BOOKS THAT MATTER

First published in the United States of America in 1959
by Frederick A. Praeger, Inc., Publishers
15 West 47th Street, New York 36, N. Y.

Library of Congress catalog card number 59-7461
Printed in the United States of America

This book is Number 84 in the series of *Praeger Publications
in Russian History and World Communism*

The editor wishes to express
his thanks
to Joan Pennell and Nancy Jacobson
for editorial and clerical assistance
of great value.

CONTENTS

INTRODUCTION

This series of eighteen articles by Milovan Djilas, brought together here for the first time in English translation, appeared in the Belgrade Communist newspaper *Borba* in the closing months of 1953. They record the intellectual process by which Djilas, who at that time was the second-ranking Communist in Yugoslavia, separated himself from the Yugoslav Communist movement after seventeen brilliant years of leadership—an abrupt and spectacular separation which caused a temporary political crisis in Yugoslavia, left a permanent mark on the intellectual history of our times, and, three years later, landed Djilas himself in prison, where he remains at the time of this writing.

As is often the case with important illuminations of the human mind, these articles appeared without any special fanfare or announcement. Djilas was a regular contributor to the pages of *Borba,* and he already had a reputation as a writer of complex and turbulent prose. As a result, the first half-dozen of these essays were treated as if they were merely another installment in that flow of abstractions which Djilas had been pouring into the nation's intellectual bloodstream since the advent of Communist power in 1945. Only on close rereading did their true implications become clear; and only in retrospect could the Party leaders trace the powerful evolution of thought which had occurred unnoticed and unheralded before their very eyes. The Croatian Party leader, Zvonko Brkic, later complained that Djilas had, as it were, sneaked up on his opponents, beginning "with considerable circumspection," and then, "as he proceeded to write his articles, sprinkling them with more and more venom."

In December, however, after about a third of Djilas' articles had appeared, and the "venom" had become increasingly evident, a certain apprehension began to spread among responsible Communists. As recently as October 4 of the same year, Tito had warned that it might be necessary to rid the country of some "remnants of the old system" which had "started to raise their heads, misinterpreting our democratization":

> Nobody wants, least of all I, to carry out new operations on our healthy organism. It would be better for these people to reconcile themselves to existing conditions.

It seemed impossible that the "disease" to which Tito referred was soon to break out in the Central Committee itself, in the person of Tito's own "successor," Milovan Djilas; and yet this is what seemed to be happening. Although Djilas had not directly attacked the Party apparatus, his intellectual perambulations seemed to be pointing in a decidedly dangerous direction.

This uneasiness was muffled only by the reassuring thought that, after all, Djilas was a trusted Party leader, whose skillful rhetoric had always advanced Party interests. And thus, in spite of the growing agitation about Djilas' heretical thoughts, he was "elected," as scheduled, to the Presidency of the National Assembly on December 27, the very same day on which he published one of his sharpest attacks on the government apparatus of which he was now one of the titular heads! In this article ("Subjective Forces"; *see* page 105), he said:

> Once men gave everything, even life itself, to become professional revolutionaries. They were then indispensable to social progress. Today, they are obstacles to it.

After the publication of this article, recalled Krste Crvenkovski, Macedonian Party Secretary, "we realized— not owing to our theoretical education, but to our Communist instincts—that something was wrong." Specifically,

> Djilas says that we do not need trade unions, the youth organizations, the Communist League, the state—in a word, nothing. What then remains? Who will carry on?

And Djilas sarcastically replied:

> Yes, sinful thought! Who will take care of [the people's] souls, their consciousness, and their activity?

And yet, curiously enough, Tito did not choose to intervene in this extraordinary journalistic exercise, in spite of what he later acknowledged was an extreme concern. Perhaps he, too, was under the spell cast by so many years of faithful service; surely, Djilas could not mean what he says! Several leading Communists approached Djilas to find out what really was on his mind. Petar Stambolic found him complaining that "they" wanted to make him into a civil servant, whereas he had plans for organizing political life around his new magazine, *Nova Misao*. Stambolic was "shocked," recalling that Tito had once said that "as soon as anyone started saying 'I' and 'they,' then all was finished." Vukmanovic-Tempo, against whose wife Djilas was then planning his most "venomous" attack, also approached him, and recorded the following conversation:

> DJILAS: "Listen, Tempo, we are not going on with this development."
> TEMPO: "That is right."
> DJILAS: "When there is freedom for the struggle of opinions, then there must be freedom of faction."
> TEMPO: "But a faction on counter-revolutionary positions within the Party cannot exist."

In late December, Kardelj had a "friendly" chat with Djilas, during which the latter stated, according to Kardelj:

> First, that Comrade Tito was defending bureaucracy, and that he, Djilas, would sooner or later have to fight it out with him; second, that Comrade Rankovic and I were in fact in agreement with him, but that we were opportunists and, therefore, did not want to argue with Tito; third, that whether we wanted it or not, a Socialist left-wing was emerging in our country; and fourth, that the possibility of the two Socialist parties emerging in our country cannot be discounted.

It is doubtful that Djilas had ordered his thoughts in the arithmetical way in which the chronically systematic

Kardelj recalled them; and yet the account is probably accurate. Kardelj reported that he was "dumfounded" by Djilas' four points. He did not, however, inform Tito of the conversation, hoping, as he said, that a reconciliation between the two men was still possible. Tito was vacationing in the Alps at the time, and perhaps not fully aware of the "terrible confusion, disorientation, and even disillusionment among many good Communists" (Crvenkovski's words) which Djilas' essays were causing.

As the popular agitation mounted, and as his colleagues grew more and more uneasy in his presence, Djilas reacted by publishing, on January 4, an article entitled "League or Party," (*see* page 123) in which he virtually demanded the abdication of the Communist Party as the ruling force in Yugoslav politics. In the meantime, Tito had returned to Belgrade and, aware that, in his own words, the country was beginning to "seethe" with excitement, he prepared to take action against Djilas; but still he delayed a final decision, perhaps because he, too, found it difficult to believe that this personal betrayal was taking place before his very eyes.

Tito's miscalculation was a costly one. On January 6, the new cultural magazine *Nova Misao,* around which Djilas vaguely hoped to rally his Communist-democrats, appeared ahead of schedule on the newsstands, with a long and frequently lurid account, by Djilas, of a tense personal conflict in Belgrade society, in which the moral character of the entire regime was strongly implicated. "One must see," Tito finally announced, "that we have come to the extreme limit." And, recounting the episode later, he said: "I had to act energetically and sharply, and I demanded that his articles be stopped immediately." A day later, Djilas' articles were officially repudiated by the Party Executive Committee, and a meeting of the Central Committee was called for January 17 to discuss the Djilas case and to bring to an end this nightmare for Yugoslav Communism. Kardelj proposed that, in the meantime, the issues be aired, both pro and con, in the pages of *Borba*. But this extraordinary suggestion—in which much of Kardelj's own interesting personality is revealed—was turned down because, as Pijade put it, "this would have meant that Djilas would have succeeded in getting what he wanted—splitting the Party leadership."

The Central Committee meeting was a decisive one in the postwar history of Yugoslavia. The Djilas heresy was discredited and the middle-of-the-road philosophy which we have come to know as Titoism was defined with impressive finality. With the exception of his courageous fellow-writer, Vladimir Dedijer, and his ex-wife, Mitra Mitrovic, Djilas was completely isolated at the meeting; and, although he made several confused efforts to defend himself, he concluded with a plea that he be allowed the right to vote—since he was, after all, still a member of the Central Committee—in favor of a resolution depriving him of that membership and condemning his ideas. Djilas did not know which way to turn, and, in his painful confusion, he came up with sentences such as: "I did criticize every aspect of our system, but I am not against the system as a whole"; or, "I do not pretend even today that these ideas are absolutely correct, although I am personally convinced that they are." At one point he attempted to restate his position—that "the Communist League is the main

obstacle to the development of democracy in our country"—but he then modified it so drastically that it was
reduced to nothingness.

Yet, this confusion was understandable. Djilas had
never, during the course of his ever-widening attack,
been fully conscious of the concrete implications of his
highly personal view of the world; and, indeed, he had
wavered even within the confines of a single article.
Furthermore, he was still subject to the emotional pressure which Tito's vast authority could bring to bear on
a situation of this type. There was talk at the time about
Tito as a "father-image" for Djilas; and there may well
have been some truth to it, judging by Djilas' erratic
behavior toward Tito throughout the crisis.

If Djilas' views were charged with personal feeling,
the same may well be said of the counterattack made on
him by his old colleagues. The venerable Pijade spoke
of Djilas' "conceit," calling his article in *Nova Misao*
"political pornography" and describing Djilas as a man
"in love with himself and his own words." The experienced
Yugoslav diplomat, Ales Bebler, told Djilas, with unmis-
takable envy, "You were fascinated by your international position," forgetting that "your importance depends upon explaining ideas of the collective experience
of the movement. . . ." The Bosnian Communist, Mija-
tovic, said that Djilas "regards us as black men who
have to do the dirty work, so that those like him can
save their luxurious brains." In this acrimonious atmosphere, Djilas' former wife, Mitra Mitrovic, bravely tried
to hew a path between condemnation and defense; and
one can well appreciate her dilemma, both personal and
ideological. In Djilas' defense, she said that there was
no reason for "all Communists to have the same opinions

on all questions"; but then, later, she admitted that she had read Djilas' articles "superficially," and that, in the final analysis, she agreed with "the things I have heard from the comrades. . . ."

Only Kardelj and Tito were able to rise above the personal bitterness of the occasion. Tito asked, with a certain tenderness and plaintiveness:

> Why did Djilas separate himself from old comrades with whom he had collaborated for seventeen years? Comrade Djilas had every chance to say all he wanted to about our crisis, and even more than he had written. We knew him and we discussed everything among ourselves, and joked with him, and in jokes everything can be said.

Tito's consternation was undoubtedly genuine; and one can hardly blame him for feeling that Djilas, to whom he had given so much, had behaved toward him with something less than complete honesty. To Djilas, however, this counted for little; for, if Tito had given much, he had also withheld the one thing Djilas now prized above all else: freedom.

Tito's personal and fatherly appeal was a strong one; and it was given vigorous intellectual reinforcement by Kardelj, who systematically took apart the foundations of Djilas' emotional argument. On the floor of open debate, Djilas was no match for Kardelj, whose logic and order, combined with Tito's restrained authority, had completely undermined Djilas' confidence. Indeed, Djilas ended up by saying that he accepted "ninety percent" of Kardelj's analysis—a good score indeed! Only Dedijer remained firm. "To speak quite frankly," he said, "I am not a robot and cannot automatically accept a view simply because of the authority of the man expounding it."

But he was quite alone, deserted even by Djilas, who announced his decision in the following words:

> Last night, I came to the conclusion that when there is a clash, I will remain with the comrades; and, believe me, it was the first night that I slept normally. . . .

The vote of condemnation was unanimous.

Djilas was momentarily shaken, and, no doubt, he was humiliated by his own uncertain performance in an arena in which he should have given his thoughts their most brilliant exposition. However, if Tito interpreted Djilas' partial submission as a hopeful sign, he had miscalculated once again. Djilas' hatred of the bureaucratic system had only intensified; and, in April, it was reported that he had, presumably on his own initiative, relinquished his membership in the Communist Party, thus voluntarily severing his last connection with Belgrade officialdom. For the first time in this strange history, Djilas was acting toward that officialdom with a realism and an honesty befitting his position. He was no longer a friendly critic inside the Communist camp, but one of its sharpest external foes, accepting the full consequences of his implacable hostility. He had, in fact, begun work on the book which was to become so widely known in the West, two and a half years later, as *The New Class*.

We are concerned here, however, not with the finished product of Djilas' anti-Communism (*The New Class*), but rather with the intellectual metamorphosis which preceded it. In a sense, this metamorphosis—representing a spontaneous intellectual progression—is more important than the neat and well-ordered complex of theories to which it led. History will remember Djilas more for his bold act of defiance than for the intellectual discoveries that followed it; and it was indeed that act of defiance, as much as anything else, that made *The New Class* an important book.

But if *The New Class* was an important book, it was also a somewhat misleading one, because it transformed an intensely personal reaction against a rigid social order into an analytical framework almost as cold and formal as the very system against which Djilas had rebelled. In this best-selling book, Djilas dissected with an astonishing detachment the brutal mechanics of Communist power—the last harsh judgment of a man who must explain seventeen years of his life before he can, with good conscience, abandon them to history. We find in *The New Class*, therefore, the same grandiloquence of style, the same magnificent oversimplification, the same historical sweep which characterized Djilas' writings as a Communist.

The problem of grasping the historical essence of Communism was not, however, uppermost in Djilas' mind in the period in which he was groping his way out of Communism's emotional labyrinth. On the contrary, in the process of breaking away from Communism he had repudiated the Marxist fixation with historical "essences," only to return to it briefly in *The New Class*. And thus, while *The New Class* deals with abstractions of human power, the essays in this collection are concerned rather with the poverties of the human spirit.

In this volume the reader will find nothing about

the calamity of collectivization, the pace of forced indus-
trialization, or the problem of raising living standards—
the normal fare of Communist polemics. Instead he will
find the writings of a man obsessed with an intangible
dream of human goodness, tolerance, comradeship; the
simple equality of peasants at work; the candor and
directness of a revolutionary army in the field; the natural ease of children at play. These are the models of
human refinement and honesty against which Djilas
measured the strict and prosaic order of Communist
progress, and found it wanting. Socialism, he said in
the article entitled "The Importance of Form" (*see* page
53), must be judged by:

> . . . moral and social norms, the established habits
> in human relationships, ways of discussion, ways
> of reaching decisions, etc. In short, everything de-
> pends on how we live, on how we solve problems
> and conflicts among ourselves.

Socialist *content* has been achieved, he declared, with
his usual penchant for fine philosophical distinctions, but
socialist *form* is glaringly absent from our life. And
Djilas had invested the term "form" with a conception
of life and orderly human conduct—governed by law,
characterized by gentle manners, open to spontaneity—
which may well have stemmed from youthful dreams to
which he would later refer in his beautiful book, *Land
Without Justice*. Certainly this conception—of a natural,
popular, lawful, and open society—bears no resemblance
to any known Communist doctrines; nor, for that matter,
to anything Djilas himself had said during his political
life. If "simple people cannot freely arrange mutual
relations . . . ," he asks, "of what use is today's ration-
alized industry and trade?"

> Once youth and torches; today impotence and ex-
> tinguished torches . . .

Throughout the articles, especially in the earlier ones, the dominant theme is the inevitable eruption of elemental human force, essentially good in character, breaking through the codified dogma and rigid social custom imposed from some source foreign to man's essential nature. These spontaneous forces need no governmental supervision, but only fresh air, an open society, breathing space for genuine creativity, and direct and open contact among friends. The theme is a simple one, recalling images of Djilas' youth in Montenegro, in which he idealized both the rough and informal justice by which the Montenegrins governed their lives and the soft, refined customs which prevailed behind the enticing grillwork of the nearby Turkish villages. Djilas presents these images with a heartfelt naïvete, as when, for example, he vaguely links the unhappy breakdown of a long marriage between two old comrades with the current political disorientation.

Djilas himself is stifling in this atmosphere. "Like most of the leadership," he pointedly remarks, explaining why he is unaware of certain popular feelings, "I have been living in seclusion in my office and at home." Communist organizations, he declares at another point, are involved in "dogmatic, moralistic, useless and meaningless discussions, *while life goes right on next to them.*" In a moment of great personal insight, Djilas summarized the inner significance of his articles in the following words in the essay entitled "Reply" (*see* p. 99):

> Both the social and personal meaning of these
> critical articles is the desire to emerge from the

> unreal, abstract world of the "élite" . . . and to
> enter as profoundly as possible into the real world
> of simple, working people and ordinary human
> relations.

During the revolutionary period, there was a direct correspondence between the "dogmas" and the life and needs of "simple people"; Djilas' extraordinary skills, forming a direct link between these dogmas and the popular movements they inspired, gave meaning to his life. But today "the Revolution is only a burden . . . a glorious tradition, but not life." And it was life—human immediacy, genuine contact with the popular pulse, an emotional meaning in the daily routine—that Djilas had lost, and which he was now seeking in his appeal over the heads of the bureaucracy to the "simple people" in whom he now imagined these things might again be found. It was not power that Djilas sought to retain, but the profound sense of involvement and need; and he had somehow grasped the fact that in spite of the increasing honors being bestowed upon him, the bureaucratic order no longer really needed his skills. Ties which were once cemented with passionate words were now held together by an elaborate machinery of state; and Djilas had become only intellectual window-dressing for that machine, for which slogans, ideology, and the passions these could evoke had become secondary considerations.

With the publication of "Subjective Forces" on December 27, Djilas' attention shifted to a more political and less personal vein of thought. But, even in these final articles, his proposals had a distinctly personal and human flavor. In spite of the pressure on him for the

declaration of a definite program of political action—
the establishment, for example, of a specific faction
within the Party—he resolutely refrained from making
such a proposal; and, instead, he simply repeated his
vague plea for a "fundamental change" in the character
of daily life, an intensification of the "struggle . . . between life and traditional methods, between reality and
dogma," and a transformation of the Party "into a real
and vital union of ideologically united men," freed of
careerists and hangers-on. And yet, in spite of his sharp
attack on the Communist Party, he continued to consider
it the only conceivable vehicle of politics and government. "Who would 'disband' the Communists?" he indignantly asked, "And in our country, to which the Communists gave back its youth and beauty?"

Djilas' steadfast refusal to bring forth a concrete
program earned him the title of an impractical dreamer;
and yet his refusal was not without a certain impressive
consistency. After all, the main burden of his attack
was the premise that the "simple" people were capable
of governing their lives according to just and humane
principles without interference from above; and that the
problem of government was simply one of providing
conditions under which this self-government was most
easily achieved. Djilas advocated no program of action
because the very essence of his message was a plea for
a sharp curtailment of action programs. The day had
passed, he felt, when one group knew better than another
what the country's real needs were. In "The General and
the Particular" (*see* p. 87) he wrote:

> No one party or group, nor even a single class,
> can be the exclusive expression of the objective
> imperatives of contemporary society.

And thus:

> There is no alternative but more democracy, more
> free discussion, more free elections to social, state
> and economic organs, more adherence to the law.

This was the closest Djilas ever really came to making
a concrete proposal for the future of Yugoslavia: "More
democracy, more free discussion, more free elections. . . ."
Only in an open society, he went on, can new and fresh
ideas arise, corresponding to new needs and problems.
In his essay "New Ideas" (*see* p. 117) he stated:

> Everything might be fine and simple if new ideas
> in their nascent state were also the ideas of the
> majority. They are not, however, and never can
> be. . . . New ideas are always the ideas of a minor-
> ity. . . .

"Only experience," he wrote, can prove whether an idea
is "progressive," and:

> . . . experience is possible only if the idea is dis-
> seminated, if people gather round it, and fight in
> its name . . .
> The true communist-democrat should never forget
> this . . . all new ideas initially seemed "stupid,"
> "insane," and "illogical."

Djilas' espousal of these elementary premises of a democratic society were a logical counterpart of his ever-
broadening conception of a free society. What had begun
as a simple protest against the petty restraints of Communist policy had grown into the fervent expression of
a rudimentary faith in the capacity of free men to govern
themselves effectively. The original protest sprang from
an instinctive revulsion against the emotional restraints

of an entrenched and closed society; but the rapid transformation of this protest into the semblance of a faith
reflected long-dormant resources of far greater force than
those which inspired the original protest. In characteristic
fashion, Djilas had generalized a number of incidents to
embrace the experience of an entire nation; and had
then merged that experience with the entire global struggle between opposing ideologies. Thus, as the year 1954
was beginning, in the fourth month of his revolt, Djilas
had catapulted his initial uneasiness into a political stance
which would soon have international repercussions.

The *coup de grâce* was not long in coming. It took
the form of the long-winded but pungent essay, "Anatomy
of a Moral," which was published in *Nova Misao* early
in January and which has become the title piece of
the present collection of essays. This essay brought to an
abrupt climax Djilas' public life in Communist Yugoslavia. In the annals of political warfare, this document,
dealing chiefly with a back-biting feminine struggle for
social position, is a strange one indeed; but insofar as
the account of this petty struggle gave substance to
Djilas' previous complex verbalizations, the "Anatomy"
proved a potent political weapon. The essay, which
combines some excellent character sketches with much
questionable melodrama, describes the "massive, icy, and
impenetrable wall" which was allegedly thrown up by
Belgrade's new social caste against a "beautiful, young
actress" whom the army chief-of-staff, General Peko
Dapcevic, had married the previous June. As a literary
work, this essay shifts from vivid descriptive passages,
which anticipate the highly-polished writing of the book

Land Without Justice to grossly exaggerated dialogue
which, as a writer, he was soon to outgrow. Indeed, there
is some reason to believe that Djilas was more affected
by the events he so dramatically described than was the
offended wife herself.

Be that as it may, the beautiful young actress, with
her glorious voice, was one of those "simple" people in
whom Djilas had come to center all of his hopes; and
the sophisticated but bigoted women who had rejected
her symbolized all that had become hateful to him in
Yugoslav society. The women scorned the actress because
she had, through her charms, "trapped" and "hooked"
the oligarchy's favorite bachelor; because she herself,
though a child at the time, had not fought with the
Partisans during the war; and because she was, after all,
connected with the stage—a questionable origin for a
member of the "virtuous" leadership of Belgrade society.
For Djilas, the lesson was terrible and eye-opening. The
wives of Yugoslavia's "great men" were possessed, in his
unrelenting words:

> . . . of an animal craving for maintaining acquired
> social status, a bestial urge more stupid, savage
> and monstrous, more merciless than any fight
> among wild animals. Look at what happened! By
> the simple appearance of a young woman, the
> social position of that clique was suddenly, fate-
> fully and incomprehensibly menaced merely be-
> cause she was one of those unknown and unde-
> serving women who not only had not been in the
> war, but who could not become an ordinary
> member of a basic Party unit, or of a students'
> Party committee, and who, to top it all off, was—
> hear this!—an actress. . . .

After four months of the most complex circumlocutions, Djilas was ready for his open declaration of war. Describing the ruling caste in "The Anatomy of a Moral" (*see* p. 145), he wrote of men who:

> . . . when not loafing about in [their] magnificent parvenu offices, moved from place to place, lived in [their] own select and restricted summer resorts, gathered in [their] own exclusive theaters and stadium boxes.

It was not the privileges *per se* that roused Djilas so much as the harsh spirit of unbridled competition—leading to a form of social seclusion—which this competition produced. On this subject Djilas rose to fanatical heights, swinging freely in every direction, speaking of a "sham aristocracy," the "pretentious omniscience" of the caste, and a "dogmatism . . . which corroded all ethical values." Everything seemed to crumble before him in this wild, journalistic orgy.

Much of Djilas' indictment was unquestionably valid; and these charges found a strong echo among Yugoslavs who resented the privileges which the Party had arrogated to itself in the postwar years. Indeed, four years later, many of Djilas' ideas—in their original language—were to be incorporated into the "revisionist" Party program which played such a large role in the breakdown of Soviet-Yugoslav relations in the Spring of 1958.

And yet, there was much in Djilas' indictment that was exaggerated, too, as anyone familiar with the central Yugoslav bureaucracy will testify. These broad generalizations reflect as much the grand passions of the rebel Djilas as they do the exact realities of Belgrade society, which is considerably more flexible in its operations than Djilas' polemics would lead one to believe.

Djilas' essay is "true," then, only in the larger sense that it postulates a type of simple, direct relationship among men—a relationship which Communism, even in its most enlightened form, automatically precludes from its daily life. In this far more fundamental sense, "Anatomy of a Moral" embodies a basic truth which may, in some measure at least, justify its exaggerations and explain its histrionics.

With the publication of this virtual declaration of open war, Djilas' fate was fixed. Although he still identified himself as a Communist, he was quick to add the phrase "and a free man" during the Central Committee meeting of January 17. Several months later, when he handed in his Party card, he would eliminate the category "Communist" altogether, leaving only the single designation: "a free man." But even here he did not stand still; at the time of the Hungarian Revolution, two and a half years later, he established himself as a "democratic socialist," a firm opponent of Communism. The exact configurations of these later stages in his intellectual evolution remain obscure to the outside observer; we know only that, in time, his conversion, begun in the months which this book describes, would be complete.

In the vast intellectual struggle which has now engulfed the world, Djilas' "conversion," the crucial portion of which is recounted here, was an event of the utmost significance. The term "conversion" is used here in the exact historic sense; for nowhere else, in our day, has a man so deeply entrenched in the ideology and hierarchy of one faith so thoroughly repudiated that faith and so completely embraced the faith of his former enemies.

Historically, Djilas' "conversion" was only the forerunner of a generalized intellectual turbulence which shook the entire Communist world in the three years following Stalin's death in 1953; and his revolt was to be duplicated, in a variety of ways, by a host of other prominent Communists: Tibor Dery and Imre Nagy in Hungary; Adam Wazyk and Leszek Kolakowski in Poland; Dudintsev and Ehrenburg in Russia; and our own Howard Fast in the United States. The sudden, unannounced appearance of fiercely critical articles, by known and trusted Communists, in otherwise orthodox newspapers, became an increasingly common spectacle between 1954 and 1956.

Yet, of all these ideological shifts and revaluations, ranging far and wide in character and consequence, Djilas' personal metamorphosis remains today, in retrospect, the most powerful and significant—even if his revolt was, in practical terms, the least successful, and even if it was, in human terms, perhaps the least justified. This is the case not merely because Djilas was, among these rebels, the only one who had occupied an important position in the Communist hierarchy and who had personally participated in the full glory of Communist power; and not merely because his act was the first among many, setting a pattern and establishing a precedent.

Djilas' unique position derives from the fact that his defiance was essentially a personal rather than a political act, achieved *alone*, within the confines of his own restless soul. In a strictly personal sense, he had nothing to gain and everything to lose by launching his manifesto of freedom. His attack on Communism did not occur, as did Nagy's, in a country in which Communism had reached a pinnacle of horror from which all honest men were recoiling; but it occurred, on the contrary, in Tito's eminently reasonable Yugoslavia, which was on the verge of achieving a *degree* of internal stability, economic prosperity, and local self-government which was to surprise so many observers.

In this seeming paradox lies the heart of Djilas' unique appeal. He was a man possessed—by an idea which could not be shaken, or for that matter, proven by statistics of economy or government. And thus it was that, although his articles did evoke considerable popular agitation, they did not form a part of a broad popular swell of anti-Communist feeling; nor could they be related to a complex intra-Party struggle for power or position. His protest was rather a streak of pure human passion, breaking from the heavens with less warning than summer lightning.

This explains in part why it was that, though Djilas was soundly defeated in formal debate by Kardelj's superb logic, his essential position was unshaken. Djilas was on another plane of human experience, where the simplistic formulae of his former colleagues had been superseded by something of far greater significance: the spontaneous combustion of the human mind, suddenly and unpredictably shattering an old vision and soaring out to new heights of expression and discovery. For these great moments in our history, on which the real progress of our civilization rests, Communism makes no allowance, offers no home, and accepts no explanation. The normal political rebel, appealing for votes and negotiating for arms, is within the framework of Communist understanding; but the emergence of a genuine free spirit, who defies the entire fixed establishment of contending forces, is outside of this framework, and antithetical to it, even in enlightened Yugoslavia.

Djilas was converted *alone;* he asked for no support from anyone (and stoutly rejected Dedijer's efforts to defend him); he made no demagogic appeal, offered no program, held out no hopes, and eschewed every organizational possibility. His conversion was for him alone; it was his exclusive responsibility and salvation. And it was, I think, this quality which gave to his act its special heroism and magnificence, lifting it above the political savagery and intrigue of much of that period. This is not to minimize the accomplishments and bravery of his more active and politically responsible East European colleagues who, in the interests of solid achievement, were forced into awkward compromises and complex in-fighting; but it is simply to set Djilas apart from those who, with traditional Communist instincts, immediately transformed their intellectual doubts into a definite program of action.

Djilas was far more concerned with the clarification of his own mind and the statement of his own new principles; and in this sense he revealed himself, in the end, as a very poor Communist indeed. And it was therefore fitting that, whereas Djilas' great comrades in anti-Stalinist revolt—Nagy, Gomulka, and thousands of others —played a brief and stunning role in the post-Stalin upheaval, Djilas deliberately placed himself outside the framework of these events, rejecting all "reasonable" compromise, including the tenets of the very "revisionism" he himself had spawned—thus leaving Tito no choice but to keep him in rigorous isolation and, then, after the 1956 crisis, in the solitary confinement of the Mitrovica prison to which Tito's political exigencies, and Djilas' spiritual development, logically directed him.

Much could be said here concerning the psychological origins of Djilas' martyrdom, based largely on clues offered in *Land Without Justice*. And yet, in so doing, we might lose the real thread of this story. As De Tocqueville commented a century ago, there is something about the genuine love of freedom which defies analysis —"a privilege of noble minds which God has fitted to receive it." This sentiment may seem misplaced in the sophisticated Europe of our era; and yet, if freedom is not to die, it must regain some of the nineteenth-century emotional splendor of which Djilas is a lingering echo. De Tocqueville's memorable statement of the unnegotiable character of liberty found noble expression in the Djilas case:

> What has made so many men, since untold ages, stake their all on liberty is its intrinsic glamour, a fascination it has in itself, apart from all "practical" considerations. . . . The man who asks of freedom anything other than itself is born to be a slave.

The story is by no means over—either for Djilas or for Tito's Yugoslavia. But, for the present, their paths are separated; and we can well understand that, when Djilas wrote "Anatomy of a Moral," he was not merely describing the ordeal of the "young, beautiful actress," but his own victory and torment as well. In the closing passages, Djilas gave a vivid picture of her grand performance at the opera: a crescendo of musical triumph and deep inner pain and despair. And then,

When the curtain finally fell, she broke down. She staggered to a sofa, hid her head in her hands, and cried bitterly.

Why? How? Whither?

Paul Willen

New York, N. Y.
April, 1959

**anatomy
of a
moral**

EDITOR'S NOTE: All numbered footnotes in the text are Djilas' own additions to his articles, and in one instance, the editors' of *Borba*. All other footnotes are the editor's.

NEW CONTENTS

Along with the whole world, we have plunged into a new historical epoch; there is no way back. We must struggle there and fight it out. But apparently everything good and evil in this world is engaged in a whirlwind struggle on our windswept soil. No hardship, but also no joy, by-passes us, "a generation created for song."

To be in the arena like this for years, under the scrutiny of friends and enemies, but mostly of morose critics; to be in a situation where every harsh word or whisper, hasty or slow action, can be interpreted evilly as brutality or weakness; to play this tortuous and complex drama for more than two decades, always expecting perfidious blows from backstage as well as from the too-interested audience. . . . No, it is not important whether it is easy or pleasant, or not, but we have proved we can play the role. As a matter of fact, we play it for ourselves, for Yugoslavia. And this role is a part of world history because we are a part of the world, and in its center, and simultaneously the center of all contrasts. The Yugoslav battle is part of the world battle. Nevertheless, it is a Yugoslav battle in its nature and its development, as well as in the way the forces are grouped and fight. Because we are a part of and a knot of all the world's knots, our battle goes beyond the framework of our country. A new, invisible battle is being fought with our forces and our thoughts, and it seems that the whole world is breathlessly following it. However, if one revolution—our revolution—should end in the splendor of a new democracy, the glowing idea of a new revolution may shine again. If the working people in one country—in ours—really succeed in retaining power in their hands, in preserving their ownership of the means of production, and in proving their ability to administer it more efficiently and creatively than do the capitalists and the bureaucrats, faith in the new world, in socialism, will become a reality.

1. Capitalism and the bourgeoisie (and a part of the semi-feudal clergy). This is the pre-revolutionary past, but it still exists, lives, persists and sucks energies from the "depths of the people," from the villages and the urban petty-bourgeoisie, as well as from the undeveloped consciousness of the working classes. It is morally supported by the West.

2. Bureaucratism and bureaucracy. These began during the Revolution as the Revolution's internal contradictions and proliferated on the soil of socialism by means of the violence of uncontrollable forces. Past and future. Moral support comes from the East.

3. Socialism and Democracy. These are forces conscious of the fact that socialism and democracy go together. Supporting them are the toiling masses and primarily the workers. Present and future. These forces

receive the spontaneous and completely unreserved moral support of the progressive masses all over the world.

These three groups of forces are engaged in dramatic interplay, in grappling. Openly and secretly, consciously and unconsciously. However, the bourgeoisie has the smallest prospect of success. Its defeat is a foregone conclusion. It is weakly organized. As a matter of fact, it does not have the support of the West which it believes itself to have. It serves only as an instrument of pressure upon Yugoslavia, and as the basis for political instrumentalities of every kind which are given their assignments. The bourgeoisie is the obedient servant of an arrogant master.

Bureaucratism has greater prospects for success, although it too is not sufficiently organized. It enjoys considerable moral support from the East. As in Russia, it considers the Revolution its heritage, but not because it was "born" in the Revolution; it attached itself to the Revolution only when victory was within reach. Like the bourgeoisie, bureaucratism is also a servant and an instrument. But it is still a new, vigorous force. And it is daily created by a socialist reality which is not yet sufficiently (and when will it be sufficient?) socialist and democratic, which is still in large measure inhumane. Victory over bureaucratism has not yet been achieved. Bureaucratism claims for itself the "glorious" past and a "precious" experience. It has achieved its victory in Russia and established its order (state capitalism) on the soil cleansed by the Revolution.

Socialist Democracy has not yet achieved either such "glory" or "experience"; it must prove first that it can win. But since two uncontrollable forces, bourgeois and bureaucratic, have arisen, and because they spontaneously join forces against Socialist Democracy, Socialist Democracy can win only if it is conscious, that is, organized.

Market, money and goods are today the measure of all things and all relations, even of non-materialistic matters. They are the economic forces of socialism and of all of society; but they cannot live and flourish without liberty. Society cannot do without their freedom. Free trade has rejuvenated socialism, but it has also poured fresh blood into the old capitalist world. The peasant's small world has once more taken on real life—if only on the surface; his greed and his inclination toward litigation have been resurrected. To the peasant, authority is once more a blind force which collects greater or smaller taxes. Living off the society by an unmerited pension, by deception, fictitious illness, falsified attestations, is now a normal phenomenon for the petty-bourgeois also. The competition for bigger salaries and better sales is a recurring, natural phenomenon of socialism.

Slowly and inevitably, the old relationships and ideas of the Revolution will vanish. After that, the conscience and morals of those times will also disappear. However, the new development is only beginning.

As a matter of fact, the West has recognized the new Yugoslavia. It has even supported her—for its own benefit, to be sure—but it *has* helped her. The assertion that the strength of the bourgeoisie stems overwhelmingly from the support of the West is no longer correct. It once was correct. Today, however, the strength of the bourgeoisie stems overwhelmingly from the economic and political weaknesses of the socialist forces. After the Soviet Union failed to subdue us, it was no longer correct to state that the strength of bureaucratism stems overwhelmingly from support by the East. That was once true. Today the weaknesses of the democratic forces are at fault. More and more, all forces of struggle are limited to their own Yugoslav origins, with the lively participation of all foreign forces, but war and intervention are less and less a menace. The field has been cleansed for the battle.

These are new forces, new relationships. A new situation. New contents. Previously they did not exist (before the Revolution, during it, directly after it) in our country or elsewhere. They are so clearly outlined, so distinct, even if they are not clear to all, even if the human being in society is not yet ripe for them.

In this new situation, all old forms of work and almost all old concepts fail. Once youth and torches, today impotence and extinguished torches. Even the old slogans, if they are really old, sound unconvincing and gloomy.

The Revolution cannot be saved by its past. The Revolution must find new ideas, new forms; it must be different in itself, as it was in the past. A new style and language.

New enthusiasm. Thousands of new generations enter into this new reality, but they cannot make a revolution because revolution is the overthrow of authority and order. Conditions for that do not exist. Only by creative action can they surpass the glory and enthusiasm of the older comrades. Without creation, the Revolution is only a burden for them, a glorious tradition, but not life. The Revolution must transform itself into democracy and socialism, into new human relationships, if it is not to be destroyed. Into creation. That is its future.

The bourgeoisie and the bureaucracy have already found new forms and slogans. Democracy is still searching for them. It must find them, and it will find them, for the sake of Yugoslav progress, which is the focus of contemporary controversies.

Borba, October 11, 1953

SOME MINOR ELECTORAL THEMES

(*On the Eve of Yugoslav Parliamentary Elections*)

There has been quite enough talk of the elections. Tito and Kardelj[a] have pointed out their importance and that of the tasks of future parliaments. At the meetings of the republican[b] committees of the Socialist Alliance (for example, in Serbia) the election propaganda's major points dealt with the victory over the Cominform, the successes in socialist construction, and the achievements of the Revolution.

On the assumption that general issues like the achievements of the Revolution, preservation of independence, continued socialist construction, etc., are already well represented in the electoral campaign, it still remains necessary to consider some seemingly less important, but lively questions, which also determine the content of these issues. In short, since these elections are taking place in changed circumstances, the concrete questions in propaganda, and still more in practice, must be different from those of the past. This election is certainly different from the previous one. There is more real and less imposed organization, more real and lively interest and less hastily-

41

improvised noise for specific tasks. There are and must be more specific questions. The general questions persist too, which is also good, but they are slowly reshaped with new slogans and are newly attired.

The question arises: since the overwhelming majority of citizens are in favor of the general matters (Revolutionary accomplishments, construction, independence), what do we tell them, how and what questions do we discuss with them?

Even Trieste,[c] although it is the focus of all general and specific questions, cannot eliminate the "little," "trivial" questions of which, in truth, the daily life of ordinary people consists. The deputy cannot be only the representative of his locality; he must to some extent represent the whole country. He appears before the whole country on behalf of his district, but before the district on behalf of the whole country. In the parliament, the deputies are "district men"; in the districts, Yugoslavs. If he is only a district man, "our man," he inevitably degrades himself into cheap demagogy and transforms himself into an instrument for intervention and protection. This is a step backward to bourgeois parliamentary forms, which are anomalous and untenable. But if he does not take care of his constituents, then he is a cog in an abstract state machine, which means stagnation and bureaucratism. The reason questions of "daily life" are insufficiently stressed in this election campaign is not because of Trieste— although like a flash of lightning, it has extinguished all the lesser lights—but because of the habits and ideas of earlier times. The role of the deputy was then predominantly formal and representative, while the role of the Party and the administrative (economic and political) apparatus was predominantly real. Now, these roles are slowly changing, which illustrates the process of democratization. Hence, those specific candidates who do not understand the democratization process will inevitably be suspended between two realities, between the necessities and demands of the voters on the one hand, and the pressures of the local apparatus on the other which, since the local apparatus is used to its "infallibility," "autonomy," "preservation of reputation," etc., will oppose parliamentary control by the deputy for some time. Such deputies will be forced into this situation if they are not active in the parliaments (federal or republican).[d]

Present circumstances being what they are, the electorate will ask their representatives to be very active in parliament in protecting and controlling organs, to check arbitrariness on the part of the local (Party and administrative) apparatus. In the eyes both of the electorate of the district and of the local apparatus, the prestige of the deputy will depend on how well he carries out this request.

The new deputy will have to be a political personality, active both in parliament and in the field. He will not get away with merely using socialist phraseology—at least not for long—and certainly not in the elections after this one.

This fact is apparently not sufficiently understood everywhere. Of course, a few wise counsels and briefings are not enough to make the present deputies open their eyes to reality. But that is not what matters most. What really matters is that the new realities, that is, the democratic tendencies, be given full opportunity to express themselves, to materialize. The electorate must, this time, be given the opportunity really to elect their own representatives. By this I mean people who have not grown rigid and entrenched themselves in office, people who have not been imposed "from above," people who have not been put on the list of candidates solely because of the apparatus' wishes and due to its subjective evaluation [of their qualifications].

This development is inevitable. In future parliaments, the new must be given powerful voice. Insofar as it still exists, the old parliamentary shell will be an obstacle, no doubt, but not an insurmountable one. The new already has a sound basis on the lower levels (in the workers' councils, committees, etc.)[e] but it was also beginning to become apparent at the top in the old parliament. There are, of course, clashes and conflicts, which manifest themselves in the minds of people because on the lower levels, these struggles retard progress—the needs of the masses and the strengthening of legality— while on the higher levels, the struggles prevent developing democratic forms and bringing those forms into harmony with the forces at the base. Even if they were now dormant—and they are in reality vital—it would not be possible in the future to avoid these "little" and "neglected" enduring themes.

For instance, bureaucratism has almost wiped out the principle that individuals should receive appointments in the administration, economy, etc., on the basis of their qualifications and abilities. Now, that principle is democratic and will have to be fought out. Moreover, in our country, bureaucratism has developed in a special way, and favoritism and arbitrariness have proliferated to unbelievable dimensions. Protection[f] is "necessary" today for everyone and everything. If you want a place to live, you need protection, and the same is true for an appointment, transfer, scholarship, pension, or medical treatment.

"Write only a few words," "If you say so," and "Well, you know me," are used frequently, and sometimes even very frequently, in conversations between visitors and officials.

It has been proved that today thousands enjoy illegal pensions, allowances, etc., all awarded because of protecting sponsors and arbitrary decisions. The best friends one can have in this country are still the two famous "witnesses" who are ready to sign anything without fear of responsibility. (And why are they *not* afraid of responsibility, I ask?) Similar conditions prevail in social insurance. Waste, profligacy and arbitrariness are everywhere rampant. Billions are thus dissipated and all this happens in a poor, underdeveloped country.

The deputy's urgent duty will be to struggle for legality and, therefore, also to struggle against such abuses. Otherwise, this class of "patrons" and similar elements will soon make him into their own deputy and turn him against the people. The people are the ones who must pay for all these illegal and unjustifiable goings-on, favoritisms and frauds. Most of all, the working class pays.

It seems that the struggle against these phenomena is going to be the most important and difficult task of the future if the deputy really wants to be a socialist deputy in what is largely a petty-bourgeois and peasant environment.

The themes are the struggle against favoritism and privilege; against fraudulent and undeserved assignments; for the unmasking of abuses and arbitrariness, not only the little examples, but the other, big ones which are rooted in the system itself; the protection of legality and the rights of the individual citizen everywhere; and political control of the apparatus. "Little" themes they may be. but very vital ones. They all concern our present and future life in a socialist reality, and not in the "socialist," "anti-bureaucratic" sham phraseology of the bureaucrat.

Borba, October 25, 1953

[a] Edward Kardelj, Vice-President of the Federal Executive Council, has been the leading Party theoretician since the end of World War II.

[b] Yugoslavia is divided into six People's Republics: Serbia, Croatia, Slovenia, Bosnia-Herzegovina, Macedonia and Montenegro.

[c] The disposition of Trieste between Italy and Yugoslavia was at that time a burning issue between the two countries. There was also in October 1953 a mass demonstration in the streets of Belgrade at the American Embassy on the position taken by the American government on the Trieste issue. It is probable that Djilas is referring to that demonstration here.

[d] The Federal parliament represents the entire country; the Republican parliaments represent the individual Republics.

[e] People's Committees are the lower administrative authorities which operate on the commune and district levels.

[f] The term protection is used here to mean "knowing the right people," "having someone in power to protect you" personally or sponsor your ambitions.

NEW FORMS

In history all great ideas, all great movements, were defeated if they did not find specific, concrete embodiment in life, if that embodiment was not in accord with the real necessities and consciousness of the masses.

This is an old truth and, like every old truth, a little dull and not amusing. Old truths, however, have the advantage of imposing themselves on the mind, of irresistibly demanding to be examined in new ways, and of requiring more profound substantiation. How are our forms of life developing? In what forms can socialism and democracy live and flourish? What is their concrete, specific embodiment in life? The answers to these questions are more important, apparently, than the answers to the questions of what socialism and democracy are, and ought to reveal how socialism should live and prevail.

The point in question is not the weapon, but how it should be used. The weapons already exist: nationalized industry; workers' councils; organized power for defending the established order against illegal overthrow; a steadily-increasing number of democratic social organizations; the international situation which, in spite of everything, is favorable; a certain level of culture and consciousness, and most important, an improvement of the economy, an economy which can no longer be called semi-colonial. Since the weapons exist, it is essential to know how to use them. The cannon which does not thunder, the saber which does not flash, only have the shapes of real cannons and sabers, but do not serve their intended purpose.

No answer can reveal new forms. A good answer helps, but new forms must be discovered through work and struggle. One thing is certain: new forms must be found; they must be discovered in the struggle for the victory of socialism and democracy.

It is well known that socialism will ultimately be victorious. That is not the point. The problem is to win now, because socialism could also be defeated. Human consciousness, when it penetrates a given social reality, and when it is embodied in organizations and realized as material power, can lead to a point where it outweighs definite social tendencies. Consciousness itself then becomes a material social force which is decisive, and acts with the irresistible force of nature. This consciousness aids the most active forces to emerge from the temporary lethargy into which they have been, and always are, thrown by every new reality.

In our country, many forms and concepts are withering away voluntarily, so to speak. The difficulty is that they have not been replaced by new methods and ideas, but by old and pre-revolutionary ones. This confuses many people. The old nationalistic and mystical concepts of feudal and bourgeois provenance come to the surface once again. This is only a transitory phenomenon, but it calls for struggle. The same is true of bureaucratism because up to the present nothing has died or arisen in society without a struggle. The struggle itself, however, does not resolve the entire problem, because differences of opinion, as well as different proposals and attitudes towards various problems, appear even among socialist forces. These are not the old quarrels with the bourgeoisie; these are "quarrels" inside of socialism, on its own soil, which is a quite natural phenomenon. As soon as the centralized control of the entire life of society—necessary and useful during the war and immediately thereafter—disappeared, differences were inevitable. They are a result of the economic system. A free socialist economy calls for an appropriate form: socialist democracy. The economy is not and can no longer be the domain of this institution or that forum, nor even of a political movement, which will decide how and where means^a should be spent. That task belongs to representatives of those who have created the means. Discussion and controversy is inevitable. Other conflicts arise as well, concerning the tempo of development, expenditures, methods of building various things, etc.; in a word, they are controversies which arise in spite of the unity concerning defense of independence, strengthening of socialist ownership, brotherhood and harmony (an achievement of the Revolution), and other such matters. Different viewpoints concerning almost all concrete problems are found at every juncture. Every committee and organization, every periodical and newspaper, has these differences. Those who are used to the old work methods and the old relations ask: what does it all mean? It does not mean anything bad. This is only what is called socialist democracy: free, open discussion within the framework of socialist forces. Does this mean factions, groupings, and the like? It should not and must not, because that would turn the clock back and help the bourgeoisie and bureaucratism. Socialist forces should and must be united against such efforts. But they also should be united in their efforts to express socialist and democratic ideas. Indeed, one could say that the terms socialist and democratic mean one and the same thing at this moment. Doubtless, the atmosphere can be achieved only through free discussion. Unity, broader and stronger than the differences, is the only democratic way. This is socialism and consequently the conscious goal of socialist forces.

Trieste[b] is a splendid example of such unity but it is not, and will not be, the only one.

Socialist controversies are not the same as the old quarrels and controversies with the bourgeoisie. Because of this, the methods and forms of discussion cannot be the same. Every discussion which somehow smells of the old methods (swearing, arrogance, trickery, hair-splitting, unnecessary impetuosity, personal abuse) leaves a painful impression, regardless of what the issue is. The importance attributed to the method of discussion must be considered one of the great achievements of democratization. Only applying such methods as internal socialist freedom, sticking to principles, candor, comradeship, etc., can make socialist forces uniquely vital in the struggle against the old bourgeosie and bureaucratism, in spite of controversies. At this point, these are the only methods which make realization of democracy possible without menacing the achievements of the Revolution and of socialism. At this juncture, these are the most important forms, but not the only ones. As a matter of fact, all forms of public activity must be new, but nothing new can arise without discussion, without listening to all sorts of opinions.

We must therefore learn to respect the opinions of others, even if they seem stupid and conservative (conservative as socialist) to us. We must get used to the idea that our views will remain in the minority even when we are right, and we should not think that therefore socialism, revolutionary achievements, etc., must perish.

Irrespective of what anyone thinks of it, even we, socialism, the accomplishments of the Revolution, the power of the working people, are today a reality.

Borba, November 1, 1953

[a] Djilas used the Serbian word *sredstva* which literally is "means" in the place of the more usual English use of the word "funds."

[b] Djilas here refers to the Trieste controversy with Italy, finally resolved by partition of the city into Italian and Yugoslav sections.

THE IMPORTANCE OF FORM

Something which is nothing does not exist, because if it did, that nothing would be something, and therefore, the nothing would exist. However, nothing implies non-existence; therefore, existence and nothing are mutually exclusive, both in reality and in theory. In addition, there is no space which does not contain something, and only something is durable. Without anything, there is no durability. Only the material world exists in time and space. Neither space nor time exists without matter, nor matter without space and time. Only nothing exists without space and time, and if nothing does not exist and only something exists, the something must, therefore, always be real and material.

The ancient philosophers Democritus and Aristotle knew this long ago. Even then, they knew that motion was the basic characteristic of matter. Contemporary science not only confirms all this, but also has proved that matter, space and time do not exist without the qualities of motion, change, and perhaps countless forms of energy as well. Consequently, motion, energy, etc., are qualities of living matter. Matter without form, space, time or motion does not exist. No entity lives or moves without a form. Forms are ways of life, ways of living matter.

Human society is material because it is composed of real people, living and dead. Ideas, thoughts and feelings also belong to the material realm because they are "products" of matter, and because without matter they could not exist. Flowers without color or fragrance do not exist; a poem does not exist without a structure. Everything great has been created in a form which is always unique and perfect. There is no content without form. To prefer one to the other is meaningless, because, in reality, they are indivisible, even if they are antithetical and precisely because of that. Anything, even life itself, is beautiful when form and content are in the most extreme conflict, when one makes itself most fully felt in the other, when, in other words, they are in greatest harmony.

In human practice, every disregard of form does not —as it might seem—arise from exaggerated eagerness and predilection for content. On the contrary, it usually results from a surreptitious, perhaps invisible and unconscious, but real intent to cheat, deceive, penetrate and coerce the content itself. In fact, underestimation of either form or content perilously reflects something else. Neither can be under- or overestimated because they are indivisible; they inhere in each other.

Ever since people have been organized in society, they have lived and must live. People, however, live only in determined ways and under socially-determined forms, or they would not be people (social human beings). These forms are in constant flux and hence continually changing people's ways of life. The biological laws of human life, those laws governing human beings as living creatures, are permanent, yet nonetheless they also change, though slowly and independently of human consciousness. People themselves naturally build their own lives in society, as well as the life of society, in accordance with the spiritual and material possibilities of their time.

Like all other things, social life always contains both form and content, inseparable from each other.

For a long, long time, Yugoslav Communists had to struggle in different and always new forms for a new content: new property, power and ideological relations. For a long time they clung to the notion that content was primary and form secondary. Though this premise was one-sided, and to a considerable extent, therefore, also negative, adherence to it was perhaps not only inevitable, but even useful, in the struggle to destroy old forms and old contents.

Today, however, this situation is no longer relevant.[1] Now, with the new socialist content already in existence, except in the villages, there is clearly no way to preserve it except by paying more affectionate regard to the despised and neglected forms.

What are these forms? Above all, they are the laws, since laws largely regulate people's way of life. They are also moral and social norms, established habits in human relationships, ways of discussion, ways of reaching decisions, etc. In short, everything depends on how we live, on how we solve problems and conflicts among ourselves. Since we already have socialist forms, nurturing and developing those forms means harmonizing the living habits (in fact, social relations) with the social base (property). Harmonizing form and content is a continuous process because destroying harmony is also continuous. To harmonize them today means to nurture and develop democracy, but also something greater, a more permanent, and more far-reaching form of democracy: it means nurturing and developing natural, human relationships among normal, simple, common people. It means stepping into a new socialist culture, into a culture of new relations between people. It means enabling discussion and criticism to be carried on democratically, in a civilized way; that is, in the only possible way for today. It means . . . it means everything: to humanize and constantly stir the content of socialism and democracy, which content is the only important thing for simple people and their lives. It means the right to arrange mutual relations, real social relations, more liberally and more independently.

Once, it was important and inevitable to fight for the content with all possible forms and means. It seemed to us that the struggle was solely for the content. However, it was also for the form, for the new forms of property, power, and all other things as well. Obviously, form cannot be separated from content; they are a synthesis of antitheses, yet they struggle with, destroy and recreate each other, unable to live without each other. Now it seems that the struggle for forms, for nurturing and developing democratic forms of life, or still better, simple, human forms of life, is our most important, most basic, and most progressive task at the moment. That task is a struggle for content too, for democratic, socialist human relations among people. Of what use is today's nationalized industry and trade (the USSR and other state capitalisms have them too) if relations are not "nationalized" as well, if simple people cannot freely arrange mutual relations, power relations and economic relations? Otherwise, the forms of social relations are imposed on them by fraud and force.

That is the way things must be. Every society, as soon as it has entered its normal and real forms, of which it has become aware, then turns consciously to those forms. Why should socialist society be different? Perhaps the answer is because form in this society should express itself more freely and intensively, for only in that way can the basic content of socialist society progress.

Borba, November 8, 1953

[a] For example, the style and language resulting from the communist struggle against the bourgeoisie and against various anti-socialist currents in the working-class movement are not only improper for discussions within the framework of socialist forces, but not even proper for use against the bourgeoisie. Once, in the life-and-death struggle, they sounded real and natural; today, that style and language sound like barbaric insults, which undermine even the valid arguments of those who use them.

LEGALITY

This story happened in a city, a city which has grown in every respect.[1] . . . A gentleman was arrested for "hostile propaganda" and an honest working family, which had no roof over its head, moved in. The family took a deep breath; life seemed more pleasant. But the prisoner's wife complained that her husband was an intellectual, no sentence had yet been passed on him and, according to some rule, she had a right to a bigger and better apartment. After all, the apartment belonged to her. On the basis of the law, the Supreme Court of the Republic decided that the apartment should be vacated for the original owner. This ruling stirred up the political factions in the city, particularly the Committee of the League of Communists—specifically the City Committee —which is composed of militant, honest people. They reasoned this way: we know this gentleman better than any court; he has engaged in perfidious propaganda against the new order and the authorities. The other family is hard-working and honest, and most important, is "one of *our* families." We have no other apartment for them. It is right that the family should keep a part of the apartment rather than having the lady take up the whole apartment by herself. Back and forth. . . . After six months, the court's decision has not yet been implemented.

From the human and non-formalistic viewpoint, the Committee seems right. At first glance, the Party organization—particularly the Committee—is right politically as well, because reactionaries are involved who could very well renounce their comforts for the sake of a worker's family. But, as a matter of fact, the Committee is neither formally nor actually right. I have tried to explain this to some Committee members and have found myself in the awful situation of defending reactionaries against communists. My arguments are: no matter what the court decision, when it is not carried out, the will of the Committee, of the Party organization, actually rules. In that case, its will is contrary to law and to the court's decision. In the eyes of the public, failure to carry out court decisions means that a power exists above and beyond the law, that there are two classes of citizens, one which must abide by the law, and one which need not. This means that so long as court decisions are not carried out, democracy, the struggle for legality, and laws are only a fiction. Perhaps my words were harsh, but doubtless there are people—good people and good fighters for socialism—who still think that in specific cases their will can be above the law.

When we have socialist property as the most secure form of ownership, and democratic laws too, then their preservation and enforcement are precisely the concrete forms for which socialist forces must strive if they really wish to achieve democracy. The laws of the Soviet Union are not bad. Neither are the laws of other countries. Very bad laws are rare in this world. Our laws are good and democratic, but how and to what extent are they enforced? In this respect, our level of accomplishment is not outstanding. Otherwise, the struggle for legality would be unnecessary, and the abovementioned case—one of the more innocuous—would be impossible. Those Communists and Committees of the Socialist Union which "lament" that they have no programs of action should be interested in that particular case, and particularly in that type of case. Observing the law is a matter of Socialist Democracy. (No other type of democracy can exist in our country.) The bases of our society contain a great deal of socialism; it is up to us to introduce that socialism into our social relations to the same degree.

Many courts and judges are bad. They can be improved only through struggle; they can be improved only if they really enjoy the rights they are formally endowed with. But if, in spite of them, another force is also manifested, courts and judges never will be either good or respected.

It is bad that courts do not secure enforcement of their decisions, and that they do not more emphatically defend legality in cases where political factors are involved. In most such cases, they suppress their decisions or remain silent. True, many provisions of our laws are obsolete and bad, particularly those adopted on the basis of abstract socialist dogma, indeed for political and propaganda reasons—for example, in social legislation—and have proved unnatural and anti-socialist. Nevertheless, it is better to carry out such provisions than to exercise power arbitrarily. Each judicial action outside of the legal framework (failure to enforce a sentence, abuse of law, giving employment, scholarships, apartments, etc., in spite of the law) is nothing more than arbitrary exercise of power (domination of political factors over legal and social relations) and represents the greatest menace to the democratic development of socialism. Abiding by law and legal decisions, however, provides some assurance that objective social justice will be done, although it may in some cases not be perfect or even just. A decision based on some other, unwritten law, though just and well-intentioned, inevitably becomes the arbitrary exercise of power and despotism. Our society longs for normal, democratic life, for normal, democratic relations. It longs for independence from willfulness and opinion. And merely abiding by the law and carrying out its decisions helps society to achieve these things. Once, after the war, "Party justice" could and did reign, and it was good and progressive. But today. . . .

If two kinds of justice and two classes of citizens exist simultaneously, we will never achieve socialism and democracy. (In our circumstances, and elsewhere, the two are inseparable.) Capitalism, where no bitter class struggle has taken place, has already created for itself this respect for law and such a system of legality in order to protect the capitalist social order and capitalist social relations from the arbitrariness of the capitalist class and its political and other representatives. Precisely due to this, such social orders have become deeply rooted in the masses' consciousness and impress the masses like a spontaneous and elemental force. Even under difficult, new and complicated conditions, this process has, therefore, proved a vivid, vital force.

Can we achieve similar results under socialism? We can and we must! We can achieve something more perfect, something which will defend man and his individuality first and, therefore, also the system which, in consequence, will be closer to the people than "the most perfect" capitalist system. But we must struggle, even in our own ranks. We must struggle against the past—past ideas, habits, forms of work—which weighs down our brains and our energies.

Democracy, legality, abiding by laws and courts as the principal instruments of our socialist system, all involve more or less the same thing. This is a necessary democratic phase of the struggle for socialism and of socialism itself.

Borba, November 15, 1953

[1] I am not naming the town because the case is typical, and it is better if it is thought of as typical. People should not believe that such a case occurred and could only occur in this particular town. Where it happened is not important for the time being, because revealing it would only cause resentment and petty debates, but the fact is that it did happen.

FOR ALL?

It is often said that our democracy is not for everybody because it does not apply to our enemies; for them, there is no democracy. These latter are understood to be bourgeois reactionary and Cominformist enemies of democracy, who cannot be allowed to plot freely against the existing order. The arm of the law must therefore be used against them. The overwhelming majority of our citizens accepts and approves such an interpretation. Confusion seems impossible in this respect.

In spite of the clarity of words, concepts and practices, confusion does nonetheless exist because of the differences in applying the policy. As usual in a class society, these concepts—even after they have been accepted—are handled differently by different forces: socialist, bureaucratic and capitalist.

The capitalist vestiges recognize no freedom which is not freedom for them. Only this freedom, freedom for them, do they call freedom for all. Each class, or more precisely, each political movement, becomes increasingly uncritical when it states that its own interests, ideas, morals, ideals, etc. represent the desires and interests of the entire society. Moreover, such lack of critical judgment obviously begins when a class or movement comes into conflict with objective developments, that is, with the wishes, consciousness, and life of the masses. Our bourgeoisie and its organizations long ago demonstrated this trait. The same is also true of bureaucracy and bureaucratism, except for the fact that they believe freedom must be confined to them, because they consider themselves the leading and most progressive forces in the society, and ardently wish to be considered as such by others as well.

Conscious socialist forces only seem to agree with the bourgeoisie and with these other forces. Yet, this may be only apparent agreement and very, very provisional. Conscious socialist forces cannot claim democracy for themselves alone, because it is difficult to determine which forces have socialist consciousness and which do not, and it is more difficult to define where these conscious forces end and where bourgeois or bureaucratic reaction begins. It is also difficult to establish such borders because bureaucratic forces justify their own arbitrariness and domination of the people by stressing the dangers of counterrevolution, although by their own pressure and despotism, they create resistance and dissatisfaction even among ordinary working people. (For instance, during forced collectivization, compulsory deliveries, and the like, who can tell when the kulak or the peasant are dissatisfied?) It seems simplest and most natural, therefore, for the communist-democrat, for the socialist, to be in favor of democracy for all.

In practice, however, such an attitude is immediately and easily exploited by reactionary forces, particularly in a country where the working class is still not very large. Especially in the villages, these reactionary forces exploit the loopholes in the law, transforming democracy for all into democracy for themselves. Consequently, they are developing a reactionary force which is inevitably treacherous under our conditions. Advocating democracy for all is only possible in our situation if conscious socialist forces simultaneously lead an active fight against reaction.

The socialist fighter, the true communist, is today distinguished from the bureaucrat or the reduced petty-bourgeois only by his ingenuity in flexibly fighting under new circumstances (bourgeoisie, bureaucracy, democracy). Thus, he strives to overcome and suppress anti-socialist forces by developing concrete democratic forms and by raising the consciousness of the masses with respect to democracy. Why consciousness of the masses and concrete forms? When democratic forms really exist and when we actually develop them from reality, they enter the consciousness, the habits of the masses, and become a genuine guarantee against both capitalism and bureaucracy. When an idea takes firm root in the masses, it becomes a concrete force capable of changing reality.

This is clear and simple.

However, the question of why democracy should also be applied to the bourgeoisie remains.[1] And applied to them in what form? The only form which can and must be applied to the bourgeois is that the law is also valid for him and that nothing can be done to him outside of the law. Hence, real equality before the law (formal equality exists in all our laws) is the only thing which can prevent arbitrariness and, thereby, the destruction of the borderline between socialist and reactionary forces.

Capitalism has already achieved this equality before the law wherever political democracy has existed. Capitalist ownership, however, makes the exercise of this right impossible. For example, the press is owned by the bourgeoisie, and insofar as freedom of organization is concerned, only the bourgeoisie have the money necessary for a professional political apparatus, etc. Socialist property, in a socialism which has already been developed and strengthened, would give preference to the socialist forces because it would deprive the bourgeoisie of the material means for political struggle. Law would also tend to do the same thing, as would propaganda, education, and the other forms.

In our country, real and formal equality are denied our bourgeoisie; it is equal only if it does not act as a class and through its class organization; i.e., each bourgeois is equal only as an individual, as a citizen. This is the actual situation. It is not ideal from the viewpoint of abstract democracy which, however, cannot be realized. It is inconsistent, too, in that there is individual equality before the law, and simultaneously, actual denial of this right to the same individuals as members of a class. But eliminating that inconsistency, as a matter of fact, leads to the abolition of democracy, to a form of class arbitrariness (most ideally, the majority over the minority). True, this inconsistency creates anti-democratic outbursts, arbitrariness, and illegality of every kind, but we must live with it if for no other reason than for the sake of socialism and democracy, to abolish the traditional class structures, methods of policy, political struggle and, thereby, all differences between citizens. The true communist-democrat is distinguished from the bureaucrat and the petty-bourgeois dropped into communism in that he does not deny this inconsistency, but instead fights to abolish it in favor of socialism. In other words, he struggles for equality for all before the law, even for the bourgeoisie, but at the same time he fights against all bourgeois ideas and against the restoration of capitalism. Under present circumstances, this type of struggle is one of the essential forms of socialist democracy.

Arbitrariness, undemocratic behavior, willful, facile and self-centered interpretation of what is and what is not bourgeois, destruction of still-tender forms of democracy, all deform, pervert, and undermine socialist forces and socialism, even if they do weaken the bourgeoisie. When power and industry are in socialist hands, then unselfishness, intellect, love of truth, discussion and criticism, harmony of words and deeds (respectfully obeying the proper laws), are more important for democratic progress than anything else, even if the struggle against bourgeois vestiges then takes longer. These are the forms which motivate socialism and democracy; they not only lead to the disappearance of a class which ultimately was able to be only a slave and a traitor, but also to the disappearance of both capitalism and state capitalism.

Borba, November 22, 1953

[1] As a matter of fact the question remains as to whether democracy should also apply to the bureaucracy. But that question is rarely posed in spite of the fact that bureaucratic domination would be even uglier and more brutal in our country than in the Soviet Union, because here the bureaucracy would be forced to strangle relatively more conscious and more numerous socialist and democratic forces.

WITHOUT CONCLUSION

Just as I was finishing my last series of articles for *Borba* (about new forms and contents), a woman comrade came to visit me. She was emaciated, sickly and old. She is in a terrible predicament: her husband loves someone else and she has decided to free him after many years of life together to which she had given the last of her energies and warmth. The usual story! But she does not talk about that and because of him forgets about herself. A migrant bird that missed its departure, she did not go south when she should have. She is too fine for this harsh age. She told me that both of them regularly read my articles, but that they had a two-fold effect on them, positive and negative. To her husband (he is still hers), they reveal bureaucratism but do not present the whole picture. What are those forces which will nonetheless insure the victory of socialism? Which are objective? Which are conscious? What is the role of the paid apparatus? Does the apparatus itself create bureaucratism? Can it be used as one of the levers against bureaucratism? They have not found the answer. Her husband is an old fighter who has no clear social point of view and is much too involved in his own personal affairs. He is wasting away in his own sick, confused, internal contradictions. "Write about perspectives! Give us clear conclusions! Many have lost perspective. They do not want to be bureaucrats, but they must be." That was this woman's request, a woman who only by her generosity has been saved from grief and bitterness.

For a long time I had anticipated that it was necessary to write and talk about actual social and political problems in a different way. I felt that the present anti-bureaucratic critic—like myself, at least—had begun to have the ground cut out from under his feet, not because bureaucratic tendencies, or the danger of bureaucratism, had ceased to exist, or because my kind of criticism was not strong enough, but because this criticism was not specific enough. The criticism did not reveal the existing democratic seeds, did not help and nurture the shoots. Now, when various democratic forms have newly come into existence, or were already in existence, criticism, if it is not concrete and creative, easily becomes an abstract and powerless denial of bureaucratism, a bureaucratism which has already become so deep-rooted that it can be eliminated only if something that is real democracy should spring up against it, and also from it (though not from it alone). The real force of this other, so to speak, creative criticism can be important only when it is concrete, a criticism dealing with reality, a real support with true democratic forms and tendencies.

However, before the meeting mentioned above, I could not organize my thoughts into a series of coherent themes and articles. The woman's noble and soul-stirring demand moved me, for with all her heart and soul she wanted happiness for that beloved man as a fighter in the social struggle, although she was unable to give him happiness as her husband. Thus, an affect, an emotion, provoked a conscious social action: this article and subsequent ones.

I tried to explain. . . .

After all, one of the most serious "socialist" mistakes in our country today is the demand that our present development be circumscribed by precise conclusions and formulas. This demand is the remnant of that tragic, dogmatic method and spiritual poverty which grew out of the brutal, inhuman, and anti-socialist reality of Stalin's despotism. Stalin was a master of formulation, of standardizing laws, human relations, human thought.

The nature of the material world—society and public opinion—cannot be standardized. The moment a state of affairs can be formulated and conclusively proved, it has already changed. Life has progressed, changed. Another and a new formulation is needed.

Description, analysis, and explanation correspond to life, but formulation does not. "Theory is gray. Only the tree of life is eternally green." Perspective, flexibility, independent and individual problem-solving correspond more to the nature of thought than "definitive" and "irrevocable" formulation. Thought, too, is constantly changing, vividly, and in the most varied ways.

Moreover, we have suffered from dogmas and "final" conclusions. Once, in the remote past, this was necessary and inevitable, when we had to break the old capitalist thinking, the old capitalist world. Only simple, invincible dogmas could concentrate all the revolutionary energies on one single purpose: the seizure of power.[1] That purpose has now been achieved. Today, another life, normal and socialist, is growing up. Now it is necessary to build industry, educate the peasants, and develop culture, democratic authority and social relations. How? All of life, various goals, etc., obviously cannot be encompassed in a single formula. Nor is it necessary. Today we are experiencing an evolutionary social development and not a turning-point when all forces must be concentrated in one place, on the Revolution, on the struggle for power. In the revolutionary struggle, dogma, although stringent, may have been necessary because it grew out of a reality that was intolerant of "evasion" and "analysis." Today, however, reality moves slowly, normally. New forces need help and old forces should be defeated.

It seems more scientific and useful to socialism today to explain, to peel bourgeois and bureaucratic layers from the mind and thought, than to struggle for definitive dogmas.

I explained this to the comrade, but it seemed to me that I did not do so successfully. Therefore, this and subsequent articles.

Borba, November 29, 1953

[1] As a matter of fact, though revolutions in themselves are the negation of everything dogmatic and traditional, they cannot be brought about without the dogmatists, without those who believe in ideals and ideas, and stick to them until the end.

IS THERE A GOAL?

It is neither pleasant nor interesting perpetually to begin with the so-called eternal truths. This must be done very frequently, however, so that other "unusual" and transitory truths may more easily make their way.

Up to now, no theory has set some remote ultimate goal which will, in fact, be realized. This does not mean that people can do without such a remote goal; however, such remote human goals are generally the expression of direct human exigencies and of an understanding of the essence of their time. Least of all did such things occur to Marx who, more than anyone else before or after him, got rid of dogmatics and prophecy about creating and setting final goals for the human race. Among other things, Marx revealed that progress inevitably forces capitalism towards its antithesis: toward socialism and communism. Consequently, for him communism was not the product of ingenious intellects, or of noble desires and goals, but instead the result of social exigencies. What is urgently required is not a goal, because goals are consciously set by men. What is necessary is a train of events, peaceful and stormy, conscious and unconscious, revolutionary and evolutionary, but like every other objective process in history, this is inevitable.

It will be pointed out that socialist militants set their goal consciously because they begin from a base in reality, and by fighting for it, they accelerate objective progress and change the very nature of society. And that is really true. But what goals are and can be in question? Only concrete ones, visible ones, which can be analyzed more or less precisely with scientific accuracy. As a matter of fact, it is scientifically more accurate to speak of a task, or of tasks, rather than of ultimate "goals"—goals generally independent of our particular wills, desires and actions, but which are nevertheless subject to objective social progress and among which are included our own actions and consciousness. Consequently, the goal is not and cannot be communism, because communism must ultimately come through accomplishing an immeasurable series of real, palpable and conscious tasks (for example, struggle for power, nationalization, steady democratic progress, development of the forces of production, etc.).

Treating objective necessity as a goal not only forces one into theological mysticism and vulgarity, but also, as a rule, results in creating some concrete task or some concrete form—an organization, a group, a law, etc.—as an absolute, ultimately-achieved goal. It then also results in presenting our subjective role and behavior as something which can establish objective laws as objectively inevitable. In addition to other things, objective necessity as a goal is the basis of every superficial and self-seeking empiricism (pragmatism) and, in our circumstances, is one of the substantive sources of bureaucratism. To be specific, some actions in our country are usually presented as a step or part of a step toward the final goal (socialism, communism). In reality, however, this is not true. Doubtless, there are conscious, organized steps which lead toward a goal, toward something presently not in existence, but which will eventually exist in time. Nothing will happen immediately except it be achieved through objective developments in which human will and action are only a part, one element in a process independent of human will and action. Perhaps this is said in a slightly complicated, Djilas-like way. To be clearer: the "ultimate goal" can be achieved only through concrete goals. For example, the goal was power, a real, possible goal. Now it is democracy, likewise a real and possible goal. But neither power nor democracy are ultimate goals. What will the "ultimate goal" be tomorrow, after democracy? Probably its abolition by its own further and more complete development. And after that? And again after that? As a matter of fact, there is no final goal as a concrete action. What exists is a permanent and contradictory progress, not as a goal, but as an inevitability.[1]

Now, when we already have socialist power and a new socialist economy, when we live under socialism and democracy—though young and undeveloped, we live with and in them—what can the real final goal be? In any event, communism. But that is a distant, abstract and inevitable goal, and therefore undisputable. Not even the intelligent bourgeois denies this, and the bureaucrat swears to it loudly. More important, however, are those real socialist methods which are in sight and within reach, those real, proper goals because of which polemics and differences arise with capitalism and with bureaucratism. Now, for instance, the new power is not important as such, because it is already in existence, but what is interesting is how it operates, democratically or anti-democratically. In culture, for example, agitation for revolution, for socialism, etc., is no longer so important today, because the former is already completed, and the latter is progressing. What is important in culture are really artistic, really new works. Etc., etc. These are the real goals. In a nutshell, the goal today is the increasingly rapid and painless progress of socialism and democracy through concrete, realizable goals, and not goals like communism and things of that sort.

Precisely for this reason, our system of collective farms, or our old (essentially Stalinist) constitution, or the way the Party is organized, and the role determined for it, have been considered socialist or communist ideals, rather than more or less appropriate temporary forms for the transition from socialism to communism. Many people have, therefore, suffered internal crises at every change of already-achieved, concrete goals, or of settled forms, as if this meant changing the ultimate goal. All those who do not consider the present forms temporary and transitory, but think of them as the absolute or inviolably holy objects of an abstract and intangible ideal will suffer similar disillusionments in the future.

Finally, what is the goal and does it exist? The question has already been answered, but one must add: liberating human toil from everyone's and every domination, that is, a continuing struggle for democracy. That is the only real and permanent goal for us today, as well as for the entire human race. All concrete forms and steps which facilitate such development are welcome and progressive. These concrete forms and steps are the goal, achievable one step at a time, one concrete task after another. The struggle never ends. That is socialism and communism.

"Only he deserves life and freedom who daily must fight for them."

Borba, December 6, 1953

[1] It is both impossible and meaningless to attempt to determine the goal of man's life. The very question, what is the goal of man's life, is absurd because man's life altogether has no specially-determined goal. This does not mean, however, that man has no goal or goals. Of course he has. He has constant and countless goals, both as a biological and social being. But ultimately, man progresses biologically and socially—the two are inseparable—according to laws which are independent of him. He also sets concrete, conceivable, and more or less realizable goals. Man lives and fights, renews himself, creates, and must do so in a given way and under given conditions. As a matter of fact, the "aimlessness" of human life consists of an endless series of conscious, conceivable, real, and more or less realizable goals. The same is also true, as a rule, of human society with this difference: that there specific laws operate.

IDEAL

If foreseeable and more or less attainable goals are not only unquestionably real, but also the inevitable result of the direct experience both of society and individual men, ultimate goals are no less a human reality and inevitability. Although imagination alone can give them their eternal radiance and unattainable beauty, ideals and "ultimate goals" are not products of the imagination, but of real social relationships and of man's experience and participation in them.

Moreover, ideals are so much a part of reality that without them, neither individuals nor society could survive or function. Ideals confirm the power of the human imagination to live not only in the present, but in the future as well. Ideals have these qualities irrespective of whether they ever will materialize. Religious ideals of all sorts, for example, never have materialized. An ideal stems from the inner difficulties and contradictions of man and society, but not only—indeed, least of all—from the search for a way out of raw and "exitless" reality into empty dreams and sterile hopes. Rather, it serves as a guidepost, as an inspiration for the practical struggle which leads to freedom from the given conditions. In the long process of the struggle, even if an ideal has not materialized, a step forward has been made if the conditions responsible for its shape have changed, and the contradiction that gave rise to it has been unravelled. The rise of ideals, of "ultimate goals," does not depend, or rather depends very little, upon human will, because ideals arise out of objective exigencies, out of life and reality. They suffuse man's mind which then gives them what appears to be their most realistic form, their most beautiful and attainable shape, under the given circumstances. It is therefore understandable that neither man nor society can do without ideals, even if both man and society are aware of their relative and ultimate unreality. People cannot do without ideals chiefly because, in daily life, the struggle in which men take part, the thoughts which inspire them, their achievement of the proximate, forseeable and attainable goals, appear to be moving toward the ideal, the "ultimate goal." And this is, in reality, more or less true, because every new effort, material and spiritual, every step forward, is made in order to lighten and perfect human endeavor. Each represents the march toward "absolute freedom," toward one ideal or another, regardless of how real and attainable that ideal may be. In any event, the reality which gave birth to ideals makes those ideals appear real and attainable for people and for society, or at least for one part of society, again irrespective of whether the goals are actually real and attainable. And the same is true in the life of individuals.

Because of all this, because of this reality of ideals —formulated to deal with a given reality in order to liberate it—ideals have a power of intoxication able to transform ordinary "little" people into giants, inflaming thousands, millions, until people consciously burn out their last bit of strength in a single moment of battle, or dedicate their entire lives to small, painstaking tasks in order to achieve that "ultimate goal" which is, in truth, another step toward the real ultimate goal. Because of all this, ideals have a fascinating, if fantastic, beauty, which cannot be experienced in any other form. They have an intensity capable of permeating all thoughts and dreams, and all "petty," "daily" insignificant work.

Ideals too are mortal and ephemeral. They arrive and coexist with the reality which "produced" them and disappear with it in order to "make room" for other ideals. Even the "same" ideal "knows" how to transform itself into a new reality in a new epoch, carefully hiding its new content, which is ugly and far from ideal, under its old, flowery and idealist garments. Various nations, classes, and individuals produce different ideals according to their own particular circumstances. But the ideals that are common to the masses and to certain other groups, are not only of interest to us, but are also the focus of general, common interest. Every individual finds in them the embodiment of his own social ideal precisely because they influence social change and impel him into the struggle.

And so, though "unreal," ideals become a powerful reality, moving hearts and minds, and mobilizing classes, nations, and all mankind for battles everywhere, for creative work and for unexpected efforts.

The difference between the contemporary Marxist socialist-communist ideal and all other similar past ideals is not that the former have had a "stronger" influence on the masses, or that the latter are not products of reality. Rather, socialism-communism as an ideal, as an "ultimate goal," has above all been scientifically discovered to be inevitable and confirmed essential on the basis of reality and the internal laws of capitalism itself.[1] Only because of this fact has socialism-communism, unlike other ideals and "ultimate goals,"[2] become an intelligible, achievable reality, regardless of the numerous phases of the struggle leading up to it. Through scientific knowledge and argument on behalf of this ideal, subjective potentialities have been developed to mobilize and direct the masses in the actual struggle.

Socialism-communism is the inevitable progressive movement of contemporary society toward liquidating its own contradictions, no matter what form that process takes.

The goal is the struggle for socialism-communism. People cannot help but struggle. At first, they do not fight because they want to, but because they must. Once they must fight, they begin to want to fight, too.

It is precisely in this fashion that the inevitability of socialism-communism, independent of human will and consciousness, is achieved: people struggle, willingly and consciously (through organization and action) from phase to phase. . . . The ideal, the necessary "ultimate goal" is realized in the struggle for the short-range, direct, specific goals. Socialism-communism as an essential inevitability is realized through a conscious, organized struggle in any given phase of the conflict (in our case, now, for democracy).

Almost the sole purpose of this separation of ideals and "ultimate goals" from immediate ones, as well as the gradual transformation of one into the other, is this: the bureaucracy,[3] like any of the former reactionary social forces and methods, sings unceasingly of the ideal and "ultimate" goal—which nobody opposes in any case—but behind this song the bureaucracy conceals other tendencies anything but ideal. The unending fuss about the otherwise incontestible communist ideal—unopposed by sensible people—diverts attention from the present bureaucratic (in our country, also democratic) reality and practice.[4] The future is promised but the contemporary reality forgotten. Yet it is precisely this contemporary reality which should be mastered and fought for, so that it may be better oriented towards the future. Otherwise, if the necessary, inevitable "ultimate goal" and the real ideal are neglected in immediate reality, they become religious myths for people, and are transformed into an abstract paradise, not even on earth, but in heaven.

Borba, December 13, 1953

[1] The socialist-communist ideal originated historically long before Marx, but it was he who established it as scientifically inevitable, the result of the necessity of change and the downfall of the contemporary, capitalist, mode of production.

[2] In reality, there are no "ultimate ideals" which can be fully realized, because their realization would mean an end to progress and the life of society.

[3] And with it, of course, traditional, obsolete, and thus dogmatic, socialist concepts.

[4] This is precisely what has happened in the USSR. It is similarly affecting our country. Likewise, in another form, reactionary phenomena have occurred and are occurring elsewhere in the world.

THE GENERAL AND THE PARTICULAR

The problem is not whether "it is necessary" to differentiate the particular from the general, that is, individual from social interests. Proving that the particular is part of the general is even less meaningful. The world and society within it obviously consist of numerous diversities. Indeed, here we need not base our discussion on eternal truth. A thing need only be explained particularly and specifically. The identification of subjective imperatives (ideas, concepts, morals, etc.) with social needs fulfills this requirement. In other words, subjective, personal and partisan should be identified with objective, social and legal requirements, thus making the subjective objective. In its simplest terms, the problem is whether the interests of any party, or group of leaders, are always identical with those of the people and of society. Under present conditions, is there, or can there be, disharmony or conflict between them?

During the Revolution there was, on the whole, harmony between objective and subjective forces, between the general and the particular. Harmony was not the only characteristic of that period, because the objective events were then so concentrated in the subjective (the organized, conscious) forces that they were able to accomplish what objective forces could otherwise achieve only in the course of decades. As is typical of all revolutions, a section of these subjective forces got the impression that they were not only the representatives of the objective process, but that they could replace it by their own actions. Today, they wish to play the same role as they did then. The ideas, morals, feelings, and even "petty" personal desires and "selfish" interests of these subjective forces were not basically opposed to the imperatives of the Revolution. The flame of the Revolution not only burned in them, but they were the Revolution. But that is not so today. No one party or group, nor even a single class, can be the exclusive expression of the objective imperatives of contemporary society. None can claim the exclusive right "to administer" the development of the forces of production without simultaneously delaying development and exploiting the most important factor in those forces: the people. This is so because, under present conditions of social property, every reinforcement of the role of political movements, either one or several, leads to delay and exploitation. The times require instead a weakening of this role, a weakening of the monopoly of political parties over the life of society, especially in our country, under socialism.[1]

Pointing out the differences between actual conditions in the present and those which prevailed during the Revolution is by no means to despise the Revolution, or to sever connections between it and the present. (If it had not been for the Revolution, our discussions would now be held in prisons, and would not concern new forms of socialism.) The purpose of making this distinction is, as a matter of fact, the following: since the forces of production have reached a higher stage of development, and social relations today are not resolved by force of arms, the methods of work and struggle likewise cannot remain the same. If people are unable to grasp this necessity for change, the result historically will be what it has always been. Sooner or later, objective development achieves its own ends without caring very much about the fate of groups and movements, and still less, of individuals. It achieves them in two ways: either it creates and organizes new forces, movements and men, who repel and destroy the old; or by a long, slow, expensive and painful evolution through succeeding generations, it removes the outmoded institutions and their living representatives.

And since the social circumstances for the first process do not exist, the evolution of the second should be facilitated as smoothly and painlessly as possible, so that institutions and political relations are more quickly harmonized with objective development and the material and spiritual circumstances of society. This is essential for socialism and for every little bit of real democracy. In short, it is necessary to adapt subjective (group, party, individual) ideas and interests to the progress of the forces of production, but this must be done in such a way that the forces of production are less and less subordinated to subjective ideas and interests.

Every social order which made possible the development of the forces of production, that is, which gave them freedom to operate in the given conditions, was able to stabilize itself even under conditions of private ownership. Only when private ownership becomes an obstacle to the relatively free development of the forces of production must it be changed; this obstacle is nothing but a conflict between the subjective-particular and the objective-general forces of society.[2]

Such conflicts are inevitable in all societies. Our problem is not to avoid them, because they will arise independently of us anyway, and society could not progress without them. The point is how to "ameliorate" and to resolve them, in order to make possible more unhampered operation of objective socialist laws and freer movement in society.

Present conditions are such that all groups, institutions, or individuals who identify their fate with that of socialism, who pretend that only their opinion is genuinely socialist theory and only what they do genuinely socialistic, must come into conflict with the real, objective, democratic, socialist process. There is no alternative but more democracy, more free discussion, more free elections to social, state and economic organs, more strict adherence to the law. It will then be possible democratically to throw back all those outmoded and reactionary forces which, because of their ideas or their temporary role, cling to the notion that they represent the whole of social reality, that they are the only "legal" representatives of society. And even if it is impossible to throw back those reactionary forces, they can be checked through the free struggle of opinion, critical control of them can be established, and democratic process made possible. Hairsplitting about harmonizing the particular and the general, the partisan and the social, the individual and the collective is meaningless. Harmony does not and cannot exist. Moreover, it is unnecessary that it should, because it only retards progress. As a matter of fact, to assure freedom for progress, no single subjective force must be permitted to hold down the other forces, and no single force permitted to monopolize social life.

Is it also necessary to stress here that this progress should presumably be achieved on socialist grounds, and that all these forces, both the "one" and the "others," are socialist, but the "one" less and the "others" more democratic? Must it be said that no single program, group, or trend is being considered here, because singling one out for criticism would only be another step backwards to political monopoly of some kind, instead of the creation of freedom from situation to situation, from question to question? This is true because the time for great theoretical and super-theoretical programs is over. And we have had too much of them already. It is now necessary for the sake of democracy to take up concrete, ordinary, daily human work, to further and strengthen the progress of democratic forms.

Borba, December 20, 1953

[1] Things are now reversed. The change from the necessary monopoly of the Party in wartime to the necessary abolition of this monopoly under socialism is the dialectic of reality. This approach is completely opposed to the usual, "normal," traditional petty-bourgeois or bureaucratic logic.

[2] It goes without saying that subjective forces cannot be separated entirely from objective ones, because they, too, are an objective factor of development, and without them there is neither society nor social progress.

CONCRETELY

All thinking which underestimates the inscrutable potentialities of the human mind, and most importantly, which
neglects the role of consciousness and abstract theory—
as well as the essential and peerless beauties of thought—
is meaningless. This is particularly true in our times and
circumstances when the brutality of the rulers of society,
or their arrogance, growing out of their technical superi-
ority over the poor, have wrought impoverishment and
havoc, as has the fact that they consider superfluous every
profound or more pretentious form of reasoning than is
required by the exigencies of the moment. Those who
imagine themselves owners of scores of nations and entire
empires—acquired either through plundered riches or
usurped power—apparently need considerably less time
for thought than did their forerunners who ruled only
single nations and empires. We, on the other hand, are
forced to think, to reason, and this for objective reasons,
because we wish to and must extricate ourselves more
rapidly from backwardness, as well as because we are
developing new social relations.[1] To emphasize primarily
the concrete and to work for it, therefore, means only to
stick to that which is most important at a given moment,

or more precisely, that which it is most urgent to secure to some extent; that is, progressive, democratic development.

In social conflicts, great and new ideas were victorious only when supported by organized masses and when those masses, through parties and leaders, succeeded in discovering and realizing concrete forms of that struggle (uprisings, parliamentarianism, etc.). New ideas have always begun as the ideas of a minority. Although everyone thinks, people do not think collectively. The ideas of one or more individuals can, however, become collective ideas. No one can know in advance just which new idea will be progressive, which one will indicate that the future life of millions has begun, which one illuminates the first sprouts of new life. In our country, obviously it is not so necessary to organize the masses for the victory of a new idea as to create an atmosphere for free exchange of new ideas. Every social reaction has begun and ended its life with an ideological monopoly, by declaring its ideas as the only means of salvation. "Even the road to hell is paved with good intentions." The first task of a socialist and every other real democrat is to make possible the espousal of ideas without the persecution of the people who hold them. Only in this manner can new ideas—up to that point the property of individuals, of a minority—come to the surface.

The true communist-democrat should never forget this, and least of all in our country, where the entire system of ideas was so rapidly undermined that all new ideas initially seemed "stupid," "insane," and "illogical."

And the same is true of new forms.

Didn't the idea of social revolution and the establishment of a regular army in an occupied country sound insane? And didn't the majority at first consider these forms and ideas insane?

At this juncture, the most important thing is not new ideas, but freedom of ideas,[2] and the strengthening and development of new forms. One must support both of them. In practical terms that means fighting for freedom of discussion everywhere, fighting for strengthening and developing certain democratic forms, like workers' councils, people's committees, voters' meetings, etc.; in brief, legality, continuing controversy, democracy.

It is well-known that material and cultural backwardness are major obstacles to the development of democracy. This is apparent in the low social consciousness of individuals, groups, and even of whole strata (in our country, this is called a low ideological and political level). But a rising standard of living does not automatically bring about a corresponding rise in democratic consciousness (cf. Germany under Hitler, the Soviet Union under Stalin). How can such a rise be "accelerated"? Only by way of freedom.

Human thought itself should determine its own limits and correspondingly its real potentialities. Every limitation of thought, even in the name of the most beautiful ideals—and most frequently limitations are made in their name—only degrades those who perpetrate them. Giordano Bruno and the thousands like him were burned to save mankind from hellish heresies. In the same way, in our own time, millions were burned in Hitler's camps to save the human race from the hell of communism. Despised and disgraced, millions rotted in Siberia only because they did not believe in the rightness of Stalinist doctrines. Ideas in themselves are not responsible for this. Not even fanatical belief in ideas is responsible.[3]

Ultimately, this fanatical faith is produced by reactionary fanatics who have a political monopoly.

The only obstacle to such despotic dangers and tendencies is democratic forms and their permanent reinforcement, as well as free thought and creative imagination. No theory can protect us from despotism. However, specific practical action concerning specific questions can protect us wherever we are: in social organizations, settlements, committees, villages or enterprises, everywhere and always. For that reason, such practice is necessary. It must, of course, be linked to modern socialist theory, and practice is essential for developing such theory.

In our circumstances, every real step toward democracy, every development of every kind of democratic form, means the progress of socialism and a further liberation of creative forces.

Borba, December 22, 1953

---

[1] Although as a movement and as a people, we live in unstable (though socialist) conditions, we do not envy governments or peoples which do not create intensive, new spiritual cultures and social sciences. Nor do we envy those who are not forced by their own feelings for meditation to stay awake nights, or those whose thoughts do not rouse them from their sleep. Neither well-being nor any other pleasures may be compared to the first (new spiritual creations) or to the second (the life of thought.)

[2] With reference to this, it may be strange, but it is a matter of fact that complete freedom of religious ritual (i.e. religious faith) would probably weaken the political role of the church. Although this freedom theoretically exists in our country, it is well known that, in practice, it is frequently limited. But precisely because of this, as a rule, the political influence of the clergy is very strong. The clergy usually exploits religion

and religious rites for specific political purposes. To prevent this, authorities and organizations limit the religious rites and so limit religious freedom. No reasonable person demands that the clergy approves our authority. Conflict is inevitable, however, if the clergy declares that only our authority does not derive from God. All in all, the clergy can preserve its political influence only in proportion to the limitations on religious freedom; theoretically, its practical political influence would be at its lowest ebb if there were maximal religious freedom.

[3] As, for example, the British philosopher Bertrand Russell thinks.

REPLY

Recently, I have heard that this series of anti-bureaucratic articles has provoked widespread comment.

All the comment falls into the following categories: 1. that I am a philosopher divorced from reality; 2. that I am writing for a foreign audience; 3. that I have begun to break away from dialectical and historical materialism, and from Marxism-Leninism; 4. that the forces of reaction have seized on my articles and used them against "our" people and institutions.

My reply, or if you like, my internal monologue:

Like most of the leadership I have been living in seclusion in my office and at home. It is not, therefore, surprising that I was one of the last to hear these comments and that I react to them "too sensitively." It is precisely this way of life and that reaction which must be eliminated. It is unnatural in present conditions; it is inhuman; it is not even socialist. Both the social and personal meaning of these critical articles is the desire to emerge from the unreal, abstract world of the "élite" and the chosen, and to enter as profoundly as possible into the real world of simple, working people and ordinary human relations. In short, the aim of these articles is to arouse socialist consciousness and the conscience of simple people, as well as that of the most progressive minds. In our circumstances, and as a matter of fact, in present world conditions, these minds can only be socialist, communist, democratic. Such a new flare of conscience, in accord with new practice, is in reality an emergence from a crystallized form: from a closed (party, if you like) circle into a "simple world" and a "simple life." And this is not a theoretical problem, but a problem of practical democracy. The problem is the greater unity of leadership with the masses, the merger of conscience and progress.

The reproach that I am an abstract philosopher is not only inaccurate, but untrue. Inaccurate, because I am not dealing in philosophy—today that is chiefly a matter for professors or dilettantes, inasmuch as bureaucratism does not need philosophy to beautify its rule (not to speak of logic or of dialectics!). On the other hand, however, it seems to me foolish to be against "philosophizing," that is, against thinking, against imaginative work, because nothing was ever created by thinking alone, but at the same time, nothing was ever created without it. If in the main I circle around abstract phenomena, it is intentional, because with readers who have been dogmatized—unfortunately, they constitute the majority today—it is the best way to break down bureaucratic dogmatism, which is itself the peak of barren, primitive and malign abstraction. However, the assertion that no one ought to take me seriously or realistically reveals that I am not, nonetheless, without connection to reality.

Those who say that all this has been written for foreign consumption only prove that their conscience is not clear before their own people. They prove that their words and deeds are in conflict. This was always, and is still the symptom of decadence and social backwardness. Two morals, two truths, do not exist in reality. Yet dualism does exist and it has camouflaged the lie with truth, hypocrisy with morality, bureaucratism with socialism.

I have no intention of defending myself against the charge that I have become a heretic of the dialectic, because the dialectic is the greatest heresy discovered up to the present, and every real Communist should be delighted if only he can be its tool. Denial is the most creative force in history. And what are Leninism, Marxism, dialectical and historical materialism? This is a great question which I shall not deal with for the moment, because it seems to me that the most important thing about those theories, as well as the most important thing to the majority of us, is their influence on the actual progress of society. At least I am capable of not taking for granted the fact that the inheritance of Stalinist dogmatism is a genuine dialectic of reality, although I am no philosopher.

I was aware that the forces of reaction would exploit my articles, but the real socialist forces could exploit them too. It is not my fault that they have been used by the forces of reaction, but the fault of reality. To be more precise, it is the fault of those who, with their bureaucratic, illegal actions and their arbitrariness, give the reaction a halo of martyrdom. They offer the reactionaries the chance to compare their words with their deeds before the masses and thus reveal the disparities. In short, the guilty ones are above all those who, in practice, mock democracy, law, and even their own decisions.

Focusing the argument on the fact that the forces of reaction have been exploiting my articles reveals only the unprincipled, if not Stalinist, bureaucratic character of that "criticism," though its wording may sound democratic, and reduces the validity of the argument to whether a thing is or is not useful to the reactionaries. It is worth remembering that Stalin falsely accused the socialist opposition in the USSR, at first condemning it for helping the forces of reaction, subsequently for also acting subjectively, and finally for betraying socialism and the nation. He established the official "truth" and "unity": the worst dictatorship in history. True, he won temporarily, but in doing so he destroyed socialist social relations, although they were still only embryonic. And precisely because it is "socialist," our bureaucratism cannot avoid being a little Stalinist, and to some extent, a Yugoslav Stalinism. It therefore stinks of the same ideological odor, and it proclaims the same "civilized" and "peaceloving" methods loudly and clearly. These methods, however, are still not directed at those of us who are "up," but at those who are "down."

Apparently there is no conflict about socialism-communism as such, but about democracy and the method, shape and tempo with which it should be realized. This is, in any event, the essence of the conflict, although it does not cover the entire issue (for example, aesthetic, philosophical or ethical problems).

I do not consider my articles absolutely correct, and still less do I consider them original. I wanted only, and still want, to stimulate thinking on the questions which, for me, irrefutably, become increasingly burning in reality. The root of these problems lies in the economy. Without a solution there, these problems cannot be solved.

Yet solutions have already begun to develop in the economy; those progress, but social relations lag behind. No man alone can solve these problems, either practically or theoretically. Tens and hundreds of people can solve them in theory and the masses in practice. Every criticism, therefore, every clash of opinion, is a welcome addition to the cause and above all to new democratic practice.

It doesn't matter whether the criticisms of my ideas are justified or not. They cannot silence the democratic struggle against bureaucratism, because it no longer depends on one theory or another, but on reality. This struggle shows in every part of our society, and not only our society. We have been plunged into an era of struggle for democracy and we cannot get out, nor do we want to. The struggle may be hampered, held back, but never stopped. I am not writing to get a good job for myself, or from boyish and childish intractability, still less from a desire for democratic glory. I must do it because, like many others, I am the "victim" of objective social processes which compel me to do so. And therein lie my sources of passion and belief. Because of that, and precisely because I respect and want open, friendly, principled socialist criticism, I cannot but have contempt for the opposite kind of criticism.

Borba, December 24, 1953.

SUBJECTIVE FORCES

Our socialist and revolutionary consciousness is often said to be on a high level, but this is true only to a limited extent. Our consciousness is really profound only if the basic achievements of the revolution and our present progress are in question: nationalization, brotherhood and unity, and the defense of our independence. These problems, however, are rarely brought up and seldom controversial, because they are, in general and as a matter of fact, already settled. However, as soon as new problems arise, we see individual consciousness searching for solutions. And what are these problems? Some of them we have already stressed (the contemporary class struggle, legality, new class structures, etc.), but there are many more (the role of authority, the role of political and social organizations, cultural freedom, real freedom of criticism, a real and not merely theoretical and verbal fight against bureaucratism, etc.). One does not see a zealous search for solutions to these problems, yet even if the answers are not yet available to the minds of many leaders and authorities, this does not mean that such problems do not exist, and that other people are not searching for and finding solutions to them. In our country, everything is too circumscribed. We have too much prescribed truth, truth passed down from above.

The point is: since socialist reality exists and is progressing, a new socialist consciousness must appear, independent of officials and forums,[1] and even against their will. Life does not wait on approval to live. Today, conscious socialist forces exist alongside official communist organizations, especially alongside and in opposition to many communist bureaucrats and forums. The conscious, so-called subjective forces are not confined to communists or politically-aware workers alone (as they once used to be). These forces also include all who stand for an independent Yugoslavia, a democratic and socialist Yugoslavia, because only such a Yugoslavia can be independent, regardless of whether these forces' ideological and other conceptions coincide exactly with some so-called socialist, or even really socialist, dogmas ascribed to one bureaucrat or another.

The dogmatic, bureaucratic theory that only communists are the conscious forces of socialism ("a special type of men," according to Stalin) serves as an incentive to separate them from and place them above society, as those predestined to lead others because they are the one group "aware of ultimate goals" and thoroughly trustworthy. The theory obscures the reality of the tendency toward building privileged positions in society, toward distributing jobs on the basis of political and "ideological" conformity rather than by virtue of experience and capability. This theory and practice must separate communists from the masses, and so transform them into priests and policemen of socialism (as is the case in Soviet Russia), and such tendencies have existed and still exist in our country.

Having once achieved a position from which they have centralized and regulated everything from ethics to stamp collecting, many communists have still not succeeded in changing their own opinions, much less their behavior, habits and manners, now that the democratic wind suddenly has begun to blow. Democracy increasingly shows not only who the true enemy of socialism is, but also that the new enemy, bureaucratism, is more dangerous than the old one, capitalism. These conditions are quite different from what is written in good Stalinist textbooks and from what exists in the ossified brains of many bureaucratic heads. Democracy has revealed that the development of social consciousness is possible, first of all, through a real struggle against bureaucratism.

But precisely because of this, these bureaucrats cannot fight bureaucratism. They were taught to fight the old capitalist class enemy which, in spite of remaining bureaucrats, they were able to do. Yet, though the class enemy's role, power and importance have greatly diminished, the bureaucrats still conduct a sterile search for them. When a few class enemies are eventually flushed, the bureaucrats bristle, which is not only nervous and naive but malicious (that's democracy!), and reveal their hidden desire to turn back the clock: they reveal their bureaucratism.

For the aforementioned reasons, the basic Party organizations assigned to each street (and to some extent those in the various enterprises) have gone down a blind alley. From the top they are repeatedly told to be active, but they don't know what to do because there really isn't anything to be done in the old forms. The themes for so-called ideological and cultural work, which committee offices invent, are dull and obsolete. Why should they be mandatory? There are long, dull discussions on inadequate activity—but no self-criticism because of that—on the changed image of the communist, on absenteeism at meetings, etc. However, no activity takes place anyway. "Cutting" meetings and mass complaints about too dull and too frequent meetings are normal, everyday occurrences. The problem is very simple: the communist organizations today no longer have that much authority, nor do they make all the decisions. The common people already live according to the new democratic forms without much orthodox dogma or discussions of politics, and like their socialist country, perform their duties and fight for their daily bread. In such circumstances, the basic organizations of the League of Yugoslav Communists and the Socialist Alliance [of the Working People of Yugoslavia] cannot have as much work as before. In my opinion, they should convene very rarely (when delegates are to be chosen, or when a change of political line is at stake). Yes, sinful thoughts! Who will look after the souls, consciousness and activity of the people? Nonetheless, living men continue to live and have lived in the world without such meetings. They live the lives of normal people and do not degenerate. They are even good and honest, and socialists too.

I think that the conditions described above put the following question on the agenda: is it necessary to have a centralized political youth organization, as we now have?

And what about labor unions?

I believe that these conditions are the reason why professional, Party and youth leaders, and other political workers, are now superfluous and idle.[2] They "direct" work, take care of "consciousness," and "inspire" activity. In their idleness, they invent and renew obsolete "revolutionary" bureaucratic forms.[3] The conscious socialist forces (communist-democrats and the people) can no longer bear these forms and those who impose them. Inevitably, the bureaucrats separate themselves from life, irrespective of their virtues, and whether or not they are publicly criticized; and life is the better for it.

Once men gave everything, even life itself, to become professional revolutionaries. They were then indispensable to social progress. Today, they are obstacles to it.

In spite of the best intentions, life has thrown all contemporary forms and ideas into a voracious mill which incessantly grinds them between its stones.

Borba, December 27, 1953.

[1] This consciousness is expressed, for example, in the masses' activity around Trieste, where the communists have only played the role of initiators, while the organization grew up spontaneously out of the masses.

[2] Only Stalin opposed this and built a bureaucratic, despotic power on the professional Party apparatus. He said that without the apparatus, we (i.e., himself and the bureaucratic caste) were doomed: the apparatus is the leading nucleus of our Bolshevik party.

[3] For example, the Municipal Committee in Belgrade forcibly and unnecessarily mobilized several thousand people for an otherwise successful and voluntary rally in Ruma. Until very recently, members of the League of Communists have also been given examinations and grades in theory. In Ljubljana, according to Golobova's letter, the Municipal Committee organized shock troops to prevent a rush on the stores for goods, the rush having been caused by the Trieste crisis. This resulted in "revolutionary" beatings of "reactionary" housewives who had bought more sausage than was "planned."

THE CLASS STRUGGLE

The discovery of the class struggle inaugurated a new era in the social sciences. The unwritten history of mankind became clearer and the written one more transparent. The mystery which for some ten thousand years surrounded many events and personalities, man and his fate, has begun to vanish. Understandably, Marx's discovery had been prepared for not only by many historians and philosophers, but also by revolutions and wars. The French Revolution first brought various classes to the fore and threw them into fierce conflict which ended with the first great, self-conscious struggle of the modern proletariat in 1848.

Obviously, Marx did not invent the class struggle. He only found it an incontestable fact in past and present social reality, a law operating irrespective of organized human consciousness, opinion or expression.

The importance of every scientific discovery is that it permits the use of the so-called blind, elementary forces in everyday life.[1] The importance of the discovery of the class struggle is that it facilitates orienting the opponents. It does not, however, give them a universal key

111

to every situation. Social reality is constantly changing, creating new conditions, and enlisting new forces. Every new situation, therefore, involves a new struggle, the creation of new fighting forms, and the mobilization of new forces.

After Marx, all socialists and progressives, many of them even independently of him, came to the conclusion that the history of modern society is fundamentally a struggle between labor and capital. Differences among socialists were rather in their conflicting views on how and by what methods the struggle could be carried on successfully. No one denies the existence of the class struggle and of class distinctions. Differences have arisen only about the methods of eliminating them. As is usually the case, theory has proved no one right. Only practice can really do this. In Russia, as well as in Yugoslavia, practice has impugned all those theories which teach that this struggle in modern society can be resolved only by force and revolution. Nevertheless, those theories have survived in some respects in the West. The class struggle, however, did not end after the revolution either in Russia or in Yugoslavia, nor has it yet ended in the West, which has not had a revolution. The circumstances and shape of the struggle have changed and are continually changing; therefore, the theoretical aspects and political programs are also changing.

It is clear why, before the war, we Yugoslav Communists took the position of intensifying the class struggle. The revolution came like a storm, shaking the consciousness and awareness of the masses to their very roots. Though we spoke of intensifying the class struggle, we were actually not able to intensify it beyond the limitations imposed by reality: the consciousness of the masses, the possibilities of organization, the means of struggle, were all determining factors.

We were able, however, to use these real conditions to intensify awareness of the inevitable conflict and to train ourselves as future leaders of the revolution. In one way or another the theory and practice of intensification of the class struggle were quite justified and correct, so long as the struggle for power was necessary, because they corresponded to the possibilities and progress of the conflict. Obviously, this intensification was also justifiable after the war so long as it was necessary to hit the bourgeoisie economically and to strengthen the power of the proletariat.

What is the present nature of the class struggle in changed conditions? And, most important, how applicable is the theory and practice of intensification of the class struggle? The existence of the class struggle today does not in any event much depend on the theory of class struggle, but rather on the existence or non-existence of certain circumstances in reality. Yet, the form and the success of the class struggle do depend on the theory. After all, the class structure of society has changed, but the theory remains more or less unchanged. The bourgeoisie is in every respect a vestige of a former class, and in the big cities, even the petty-bourgeoisie is gone.[2] Continuing the struggle against the bourgeois reactionaries exclusively on a theoretical basis and "line," and not on the basis of law, must now deviate into bureaucratism, into conflict with plain people because they hold differing opinions, or because of their frequently justified grumbling and objection to artificially imposed tasks.[3]

And more important, the enemy of socialism and

democracy is not only the bourgeoisie, but also that bureaucratism which constantly violates the law and wishes to exert ideological and political power over the people in order to exploit them. It often invents enemies merely to justify its own existence and to express its own loyalty, a loyalty to itself and to its ideology.

The stories about intensifying the class struggle above the law and in spite of the law undermine legality and democracy. There is no need to intensify or attenuate anything according to a preconceived ideological pattern. We must follow reality, adopt laws, and then obey them. We must fight only where the class enemy exists and only by means not forbidden by law.

The duty of the state organs (primarily of the courts, the UDBA [political police] and the police) cannot be intensification of the class struggle, but must instead be preservation and implementation of the law. In my opinion, these organs must rid themselves of Party interference especially in those outlying districts where it is prevalent. Otherwise, even with the best intentions, they cannot avoid being undemocratic and unduly influenced by dogmatic ideological and political considerations, as well as by local interests. They must become representatives of the state and of the law, thereby of the people, rather than representatives of the political interests and conceptions of one political organization or another. These are the inevitable results of the struggle for legality and democracy, and a step forward. If these officials continue to intensify the class struggle by disregarding the law, they must inevitably give special favors to those who share their opinions, and whom they consider sympathetic and "trustworthy." By using these same criteria, they must also inevitably judge the virtues of other citizens, and so divide them into lower, non-Communist and higher, Communist classes. The class struggle is, in fact, intensified by such "theory" and practice. In so doing, they may appear to be distinguishing between socialism and capitalism, but actually they are working against the people.

In our country, only a democracy which continually makes progress can clarify class conflicts and diminish class differences.

Borba, December 31, 1953

[1] After becoming acquainted with the laws of electricity, people built power stations and transmission lines, and new lights flared. However, people cannot invent or change natural laws. They cannot, therefore, reduce or increase electrical, or any other kind of energy; they can only use these energies to the extent to which they extract them from nature.

[2] They exist, and in great numbers insofar as thought is concerned, but they are not as numerous and important as a social stratum. They are almost all private merchants, private employees, or the like, or they are in the socialist network. The number of private artisans is small.

[3] Not long ago, all the papers reported the trial of a worker who listened to BBC and who did not like to take part in labor brigades. The court acquitted him, but its exoneration was meaningless. The verdict was that he needed further political indoctrination. Is it the task of our courts to weigh the people's political consciousness? How long will we read of ideological sentences in place of legal ones? How long will sentences be pronounced on the basis of dialectical and historical materialism, and not on the basis of law? What kind of security organs are these which even in the center of Belgrade dare today to bring such a man before the court?

NEW IDEAS

Everything would be fine and simple if new ideas in their nascent state were also the ideas of the majority. They are not, however, and never can be. In fact, if they were from the beginning the ideas of a majority, they would not be new ideas at all.

New ideas are always the ideas of a minority. Historically, they always have been and they always will be, as much because of the nature of the relationship between human thought and reality as because of the nature of human thought itself. Every new idea, if it is really new, reflects some new reality, some change either in the material world, or in scientific discovery or artistic creation. Restless, relentless reality constantly impinges on the human mind which must react to it in order to explain, adapt and "lead" it. Neither society nor the individual could survive if they stopped thinking, stopped seeking adjustment to reality, stopped explaining it and struggling within its confines. A human being lives only when he struggles (by working) and when he thinks (by explaining reality and adjusting to it). The less he is able to function in society and in reality, the closer he is to death as a social being, as a man. Roughly speaking, this is as true of classes and social strata as it is of individual ideological groups. They, too, live when they discover reality, but when they lose it, they die.

New ideas do not appear of themselves; they are the result of the inevitable progress of society, of the social struggle, as well as of man's struggle with nature. They are the result of the uninterrupted, unbreakable and contradictory relationship between reality and human effort. Reality is constantly changing and human beings must explain these changes by thinking them through so that they can influence the changes and so be able to live and progress in the new conditions.

Human beings can only live collectively, in society, yet as a society they are divided into opposing groups and classes, with divergent interests, ideas, etc. However, they are not conscious of living collectively: they think as individuals, personally, though of course not "purely" individually, but as individual members of a society. They think as individuals who, roughly speaking, represent not only themselves but also a specific class, stratum of society, or interest. Whether the new ideas are political, scientific or artistic, they are formulated by individuals, or at best by groups, never in their own names, but in the name of some segment of society. A new idea in the minds of human beings must manifest itself because social reality demands it, and that the idea occurred to one individual or another is fortuitous.

However, all these simple, natural phenomena are complicated in society because new ideas represent new social forces, a rising social reality which tends to drive out the existing one in its attempts to secure for itself the "right to live." At first, the old forces resist, always ideologically, protesting that the new forces' ideas are bad. They claim that the new forces are harmful, heretical, immoral and anarchic with respect to the existing society, and to the established moral and other norms. Actually, the new ideas are precisely those things with respect to the old ones, otherwise they would not be new, but old ideas. The old ideas and relationships are denied by the new morals, relationships and organizations, but for the sake of new, higher morals and better relationships.

This ideological struggle is an intellectual picture of a real struggle which is not quite so apparent. The ideological struggle is, as a matter of fact, the struggle of various social forces transposed into human minds.

In such a relationship between old and new, the representatives of the old ideas and obsolete social relationships treat the new ideas and their representatives with "prejudice" and "without objectivity." This "lack of objectivity" and this "prejudice" are due not only to the fact that the old order represents conservative, "selfish" interests and inherited or usurped rights which have been turned into unjust privileges, but also due to the fact that the old ideas and concepts are unable to comprehend the new reality and the new movement. The new concepts and categories seem monstrous to them, immoral and unnatural, since they obviously differ so much from what is old and traditional. In reality, however, the old concepts have become unnatural, for their forms can no longer contain and accommodate the new reality and the new relationships.

No one can know in advance the extent to which an idea is new and progressive. Its worth can be proven only by experience. Such experience is possible only if the idea is disseminated, if people gather round it and fight in its name. That is why the old, resisting forces always try to have new ideas "forbidden" as a means of preventing their dissemination. Conversely, new ideas and forces always seek free exchange of ideas, equality and freedom in the ideological struggle. Moreover, since the new ideas are more truthful and vital than the old, they can allow themselves the "luxury" of being more tolerant, principled and generous: they can avoid disloyalty, immoral methods, etc. This is understandable because life and victory lie ahead of them.

The old ideas are still dominant among us, more dominant than one would suppose. We have received a substantial part of socialist ideas and theories not only in Leninist form but in the Stalinist form of Leninism (for example, the theory of the Party, and a great deal of the theory about the state too). As long as our practice was predominantly bureaucratic, or tended to be bureaucratic, we were able to use these ideas. Although the Revolution did not fundamentally "agree" with these ideas, nor these ideas with it, later in the bureaucratic reality, these ideas attained a more solid footing. Our practice and the ideological struggle have broken Stalinist ideology as a whole, but they have not destroyed it. It still lives in the minds of man, but not, of course, as Stalinism. Stalinism among us has become synonymous with Cominformism, that is, with betrayal of our country and of socialism. It lives as "Marxism," "Leninism," etc.—the sum of inherited and formulated ideas and rules, with their corresponding organizational, political and other forms. It is not important whether or not these ideas have become obsolete; more precisely, the crucial question is whether the practice in whose name they speak has become obsolete.

Only in a free struggle of ideas is it possible to discover in our country—without a major social upheaval —which ideas and concepts are old and which new but also, and more important, which are the valid forms of life. An ideological struggle is also necessary because one set of ideas always misrepresents the other. Our older ideas will always call the new ones "anarchist," "petty-bourgeois," and "Western," while the new ones will call the old "bureaucratic," "Stalinist," and "despotic." Meantime, the truth can be discovered only by experience, in struggle. The more this struggle is conducted on free and equal terms, the more one can talk about the real, if only newly-born, democratic relationships. Often, the truth is somewhere in between. If a discussion has really been free and principled, the truth is not usually all on one side, at least not the whole truth.[1]

Borba, January 1, 2, 3, 1954

[1] At the request of the editor of *Borba,* Comrade Milovan Djilas has agreed to write an article for the January 4th issue which will explain in greater detail the views he previously enunciated in his article "Subjective Forces."

LEAGUE OR PARTY

This article is a little different: the discussions provoked by my article, "Subjective Forces," because it was said that the article dealt too extensively with concrete and specific matters, prompted me to formulate my views on the problem in question in a more detailed and definite way. The aforementioned article does not differ—except in its specificity—from the other articles I published previously in *Borba*. Individual paragraphs notwithstanding, the articles represent an overall view, one and the same conception for practical as well as for more "complicated" theoretical questions. And since we have accepted the functionaries' opinions as "directives," particularly where specific work methods are concerned, I must emphasize, although it is clear from my articles, that no forum stands behind my opinions except me, personally. This is also true of the opinions I expressed in "Subjective Forces." Consequently, my opinions in these articles are not "directives," but merely a statement of views, materials for discussion and consideration. This work method and statement of views is new and that alone confirms the fact that a change of real relations has already begun in our country, and with it, too, a change of work methods.

All I am now writing, therefore, is merely repetition of what I have already said, but in more concrete and condensed, though more specific form.

The formal aspect of the questions: Marxists have never shown much respect for resolutions, which does not mean that they have underestimated their importance, though few resolutions, at least in the history of the working-class movement, have been realized. Resolutions are, in reality, actual pictures of the future, summaries of experience, techniques of mobilizing, points of orientation, but ordinarily life flows on its own course outside of them, and fundamentally that must be understood.

Nonetheless, I consider the question of my proposals about changing the work inside the League of Communists to conform entirely to the Sixth Congress decisions and the Statute approved by it as serious and as yet unresolved. My opinions seem to me to conform to those decisions though some of my proposals may not conform to the letter of the Statute. If the Sixth Congress decisions mean weakening the political-practical role of the League of Communists as a party,[a] and strengthening its ideological and educational role, as well as strengthening the political-practical function of the Socialist Alliance,[b] then my opinions are identical with them. This cannot be said, however, for those practices which "strengthen" the League of Communists by imposing the form and content of ideological work, particularly ideological work which has no connection either with theory or reality. This is also true of interference by Communist organizations in all things, while all serious and systematic

124

work of the Socialist Alliance is simultaneously neglected and treated as less valuable.

Although it is only the formal, and for me secondary aspect of the problem, I remember how the Central Committee of the Yugoslav Communist Party changed essential parts of the Statute approved by the Fifth Congress during the period between the Fifth and Sixth Congresses. And the Central Committee acted well and wisely. Life had broken the accepted traditional forms and the Central Committee adapted itself to the earthly Kingdom and not to that of the wise Stalinist Bibles. In this case, however, that is not necessary. The Statute approved by the Sixth Congress is, fortunately, and by no means fortuitously, flexible enough to make possible organizational changes "even" in the ways I have stressed.

Even if that were not so, solutions would have to be found when the necessities of life called for them. Consequently, I do not believe it essential whether one detail or another conforms to the Statute, although that must always be taken into consideration; what is essential is whether the detail strengthens or weakens socialist forces and democracy.

The actual situation in the urban organizations is this: initiative in the new work methods increased among the membership after the Sixth Congress, but the committees have only slowly and "under pressure" accepted the new methods. The committees, therefore, blame the inactivity of the urban organizations, and as a matter of fact, the actual methods of work and principles of organization make real activity impossible. The actual work methods in the League of Communists (in the basic organizations and lower-echelon committees) were not developed, but remain basically the same as before the Sixth Congress: the apparatus plans and fixes everything in advance. The communists separate themselves from the socialist mass of ordinary citizens, the organizations get involved in dogmatic, moralistic, useless and meaningless discussions, while life goes right on next to them.

Crisis in Forms of Work: The presumption that the contradictions between life and the forms of work and the absence of work capacity among communist organs are the result of "the low political level of the basic organizations," or the fact "that the committees cannot find their way," and similar reasons, are not based on real scientific, political analysis.

Our best men—those who were withdrawn from the institutions and who are better than the people on the committees—are now in the urban basic organizations. But those same organizations, committees and men who, when they were on a high level, were more or less able to solve all problems, now have the feeling of futility and do not quite know what to do. Obviously, the problem lies not in them—at least not entirely in them—but elsewhere.

It is striking that the crisis in our methods of political work has emerged for the most part only in the most highly-developed centers (the big cities) and in the most highly-developed organizations.

For me, the crux of the entire problem lies precisely in that: the city is already quite socialist and democratic, and therefore does not permit obsolete methods because economic and political life has become freer. Moreover, only those to whom these obsolete methods are applied can be aware of them, and can observe the discrepancy between the methods and the change in reality. The situation in the villages is different; there, economic and social changes are not as great and cannot even approximate those in the cities. The discrepancy between reality and method, therefore, is not felt so much there, which does not mean that it is nonexistent in the villages and that changes will not be necessary there too. However, they are not so urgent, nor need they be so radical.

New economic relations and increased urban democratic consciousness no longer tolerate old political methods and relations. Formerly, the Party Committee kept all the power in its own hands, even administered the people's consciousness, ordered how and what things were to be "done," and it was responsible for the ideological and political level. But even in such circumstances the people's consciousness was not strengthened by good speeches and articles alone, but by life as a whole. Because life then was considerably less socialist than now, it was necessary to "elaborate" the theory further. We were then involved in a different struggle, and unity in everything, even in accepting imposed ideas, was consequently unavoidable. But that is no longer true, or at least should not be true. Socialism in the cities is now stronger than capitalism. If one takes into consideration the fact that communists no longer have their old power, that they no longer administer everything, that they now have new methods—because they live under new conditions and relations—it is obvious that the old political and ideological work methods must handicap them.

And that is the case. The crisis in the method and character of political and ideological work originates not only in our usual, and in our practice so frequent, discrepancy between work methods and reality, but is now much more profound. The change in the economic and social structure has caused and is still causing other changes. The increase of economic freedom conflicts with the old relations and ideas. Our entire inherited ideological and organizational system and apparatus (except the basic materialistic, Marxist, philosophical and sociological premises) are now called into question. The actual discrepancy between work methods and reality can and must be eliminated, but it is more profound than usual: a fundamental change is at stake. Theoretical elaboration, the explanation of new phenomena, cannot occur overnight, all of which causes hitherto unknown difficulties, but that does not mean that ideology is not related to organization, or that ideological problems and organizational ones can be resolved separately. Theory and practice are connected, but they are always connected regardless of the fact that the methods change and that different terms are required for different methods.

That problem will take longer. How long it takes is not important, but what is important is that its nature be understood and the expression of its internal contradictions be facilitated. Accordingly, there are not nor can there be radical changes, but only a normal socialist progress which cannot come about without conflicting opinions.

The crisis in work methods is an expression of the inability to understand the new characteristics, an expression of the old methods' resistance to the new methods and characteristics. Today, a struggle is going on between life and traditional methods, between reality and dogma. Once, these old methods were neither formal nor dogmatic, but because they are no longer relevant today, they are now in basic contrast to what they were before. They are a pattern and a dogma divorced from life and, under our specific circumstances, they must appear as bureaucratic resistance to democracy and as state capitalism opposed to socialism, even if the individuals who in their subconscious minds embody these tendencies are opposed to both dogmatism and bureaucratism. That means something, because it exists in reality, and when something begins to fall behind reality, it must manifest itself in an ugly form. How beautiful was youth once! . . .

"Dissolution" of the League of Communists: Of all the ridiculous suggestions I have recently heard, this is one of the most absurd. Who would "disband" the Communists? And in our country, to which the Communists gave back its youth and beauty? As long as Communists want to have their organization, they will have it; so it has been in the past and so it will be in the future.

The question is, therefore, not whether the Communist League should continue or not, but what its organization and work should be like. In this respect, however, the old Communist Party was not always static. It changed its methods of struggle and its technical organization. The question now is, I think, not to carry out a "temporary," minor, tactical and organizational change, but, once again, to change something more profound and essential. The problem is whether the League of Communists is to remain the Party in the old, prewar, pre-Cominform and post-Sixth Congress sense, or not. Such a change would be incomparably greater and more fateful, however, than the changes in method in the old Yugoslav Communist Party. Such a change, therefore, requires a more cautious approach, imposes a need for much more careful thought and discernment, and demands considerably more courage than all those changes we carried out in the old Party.

Facts and experience teach us: first, the League of Communists is no longer the old Communist Party, not only because everything is no longer centralized in its hands, and it no longer controls everyone and everything, but also because its membership is different, much broader in social origin and in the ideas inherited. Secondly, the burden of the battle against the Cominform was carried by the communist old guard, ideologically and morally steeled and faithful to principles, and by the masses of the people. One part—and by no means a small part—of the Party membership remained without initiative, in that it outwardly agreed to and slowly accepted as a matter of routine the new doctrines and the new criticisms of the Soviet Union and bureaucratism on one hand, and on the other, mired in its own Cominformist ideological conservatism, hindered the agreement concerning the supply of Western arms, a vital issue for our country. (Mention should also be made here of the fact that among the Cominformists arrested, there were no ordinary citizens, only Party members and, though rarely, some so-called sympathizers.) Thirdly, the Trieste crisis has demonstrated beyond our expectations the unity [of our people] in defense of our country. This is more, not less, significant than the fact that socialist Yugoslavia has been consolidated internally and externally, and that its further progress and external strength depend on whether it remains consistent to its ideals; in short, how much it remains socialist and democratic. (It follows from this that we no longer call those citizens "enemies" and "traitors" who voluntarily and conscientiously defend and stand up for their country, nor can we treat them contrary to and in spite of the law.) Fourth, the last elections proved that the Socialist Alliance, with the communists as its core (and not as a political faction!), can successfully fight contemporary political battles. The elections have further shown that the classical, bourgeois urban forces of reaction have remained passive and impotent, while the subjectivism and arbitrariness of the political apparatus (particularly, I think, the Party-member section of the apparatus) has greatly asserted itself. Fifth, and this is most important, socialist consciousness is no longer the exclusive domain of, nor represented solely by, communists and their speeches and writings. It is held in common with the communists by broad sections of the society in different forms and intensity, beginning with the struggle for defense of the country, which the immense majority of citizens have in their consciousness, through the teachers who educate the children in this for this country, up to the writers, painters, scientists and Marxist theoreticians. (And once only we communists were consciously for socialism.)

To be brief, one may say that before and during the war, the Yugoslav Communist Party was the revolutionary party of the working class and of the revolutionary intellectuals. Because of the long duration of the war, and particularly afterward, the Party has increasingly taken on "the garb of the peasant and clerk," so to speak, which has correspondingly changed its internal life.

I do not mean to say by this that the League of Communists is "better" or "worse" than the Yugoslav Communist Party, but only that they are no longer, and can no longer be, the same organization. Regardless of these things, one fact stands out indubitably; that the Communist Party up to the time of its taking a clear-cut anti-bureaucratic position (which coincides approximately with its transformation into the League of Communists) was attractive to many people because it was the ruling party and, thus, membership in it, though this did not result in special privilege, was a certificate of trustworthiness and a recommendation with which one could more easily find a job. One could not say the same thing of the Communist Party either before or during the war. In those days, few people aspired to Party membership. During the so-called bureaucratic era, however, membership increased overnight. What is the situation today? Today we see that membership not only is not increasing, but is decreasing. It is not important, of course, whether this phenomenon is "good" or "bad." What is clear to me, however, is that in the present circumstances the old work methods cannot remain the same, and that, alas, many of both the inherited and newly-acquired ideological and political doctrines must share this same fate.

The old, pre-revolutionary and revolutionary Yugoslav Communist Party no longer exists in fact. What has survived is its positive revolutionary heritage and its old cadres, its communists and the masses. No matter how great our nostalgia is for the old Party, we must reckon with the facts, with people, and we must consider what we have to do in these changed circumstances, and how we are to do it.

The battle for democracy and against obsolete forms of society and outmoded methods of thought must be fought by the communists, by those trained and experienced cadres who, through sleepless nights and efforts beyond human endurance (physical and mental collapse, and even death), have shouldered and carried the heaviest burdens during the reconstruction period (I include here such tasks as compulsory food collection from the peasants, the building of industry, the struggle with Cominformism). Only such people, disinterested, imbued with the spirit of sacrifice, modest and discreet, as we knew them in the revolutionary days, are fit to carry on this battle. Only people who do not look on democracy and socialism through the prisms of their own personal interests, but instead see in the achievement of socialism the fulfillment of their own personal happiness, are capable of being and remaining pillars and driving forces in this process of our democratic transformation and re-education. There can be no democracy in our country without communists, and without their active and leading collaboration. Their leading role must somehow become manifest in the organizational setup of the nation as well. If it could have been done without them, it would already have been done. Without communists there would be no Yugoslavia. This does not mean, however, that the communists should be organized and work in the old pattern, for neither the old organizational forms nor the old methods were anything more to the communists than means to achieve their final goals: the destruction of bourgeois power, the expropriation of the exploiters, etc. Socialism and democracy can be built only of the construction material we acquired in our Revolution. This is not bad material. It has withstood terrible pressure and devastating fire. These pressures and fires no longer perturb us: they are past.

New Methods of Work: The conditions in which we must work have changed. Our socialist economy is more or less free. The socialist consciousness of our towns is on the rise. Against the enemies of socialism we are now able to use the law as a sufficient means of physical enforcement, while in the political field, propaganda and agitation seem powerful enough to achieve their ends. On the other hand, Stalinist ideology and practice, including the Party apparatus' monopoly over the ideological, political and other activities of man, are everywhere breaking up. In these changed circumstances, the basic organizations of the League of Communists have nothing left to do along the old Party lines in the cities, because they no longer control directly either political or economic life. There is hardly anything for the old professional Party officials to do, and still less for the youth functionaries. It would be untrue and inhumane to deny today the enormous contribution of old Party officials in the past, or to say that we could have achieved all our democratic aims without them. No, without them, all our democratic aims would be empty dreaming and the thrashing of chaff. But one must agree that salaried Party officials are a thing of the past. By this I do not mean to say that society has no moral obligation to take care of the old officials. They have sacrificed their youth, health, and education in order to enable us to achieve the form of society we now have.

Yes, communists, real communists, who are revolutionaries and democrats, will be more and more necessary in the future, but what I think are no longer necessary are some of the precisely circumscribed methods and functions, or the limitations of those methods and functions, inside and outside the League of Communists. The roots of the evil are in the present organizational structures, and in the style and methods of work. Old concepts and methods continue to be applied in new circumstances when the masses of communists, and of the people, for that matter, can now influence decisions more directly.

That is why the present methods in the activities of the urban basic organizations are not only barren of results, but have also become a direct obstacle to more productive and creative activity among communists themselves, an obstacle to shaping and perfecting their own personalities, an obstacle in the communists' struggle for democracy, an obstacle to their useful collaboration in the political and national life of the country. Present methods are a handicap to the communists because these methods waste their precious time, kill their incentive to work, and are a source of confusion to their consciences. The final aim of a true communist is not, and cannot be, some kind of abstract party as such, catering exclusively to communists; it is, instead, elevating the people's socialist consciousness, educating the masses for democracy, and formulating concrete means of fighting for democracy, legality, the rights of citizens, etc. That is why I think communists may now discuss current problems within the Socialist Alliance; that is, not first in the League of Communists and only then, after they have been debated there, "passing them on."[1]

It is not my purpose to propose work methods, but because we are dealing with that problem, let me have my say in that as well. The meetings of the basic organizations of the League of Communists are neither necessary nor useful if problems of daily political work are the only thing on the agenda, and unless there are some special problems (important political changes or political danger), these meetings should not take place. It is useful and necessary, however, for communists to join the Socialist Alliance as ordinary members, and to work.

And after that, what remains of the basic organizations of the League of Communists? The election of leaders and delegates, plus exceptional work, and something very important, more important than everything else: internal ideological work. This is the most sensitive point because people cannot tolerate it or be enthusiastic when they are ordered about and treated as immature human beings. Life can be organized only on the basis of personal desires and complete voluntarism. Such a life cannot be imposed on any one. The only possible method is lecture and perhaps discussion, because it is voluntary and adjusted to the desires and spiritual level of the audience. But it should not be restricted to communists: it should be public and available to all who are interested. Lectures may vary, ranging from the most abstract theories and analyses of current political events to cultural, scientific and educational subjects. In that way we would break down the ideological differences between communists and other citizens, granting no special privileges to either. And most important, the personality of the communist will be respected.

Thus, the League of Communists would change from the old Party into a real and vital union of ideologically united men. Careerists and opportunists would lose their interest in Party membership overnight. The struggle for Party purity, for the image of the pure communist, etc., would also cease overnight. The ones who were not "pure" would quit by themselves or become "inactive," because no personal advantages would accrue to them except communist idealism, and only the real communists would have that. Communists would be active everywhere they live and act as citizens. The number of communists in various organizations would be small, but they and their ideas would be diffused throughout. No one would "control" their activities or "line," and no one would give them "directives." Moreover, on the basis of lectures and theses discussed, they would take their stand on local issues, social life and the unsolved problems of their own life and work.[2]

The present League of Communists would "weaken," "wither away" as a classical party, and on the other hand, the conscientious role, comradeship and true discipline of pure communists would be strengthened. The League of Communists would gradually take on the character of a strong, ideological, widely-diffused nucleus, but would lose its party character. It would merge with the Socialist Alliance, and the communists would merge with the ordinary citizenry. Why should that be bad for communists and socialism? On the contrary, the Socialist Alliance would become a truly socialist factor and would not be a self-appointed élite of communists. The role of personality would grow, on the basis of its quality and its function among the masses, and not only on the basis of its position in the Party Committee or administration. The direct political role of the masses would also grow so that the people would decide most political problems by themselves and without imposed, patented and enforced leadership and formulae. Thus, the good, talented communists would become ideological and political leaders, though not very quickly or easily. Without either regular attendance at dull and meaningless meetings, or ideological indoctrination, it would become clearly known very quickly who was a *de facto* communist, preferring the people, democracy and socialism more than his own personal advantage.

By the way, I might mention that in our country, learning by rote, repeating what some authority has "wisely" said, or acquiring a schoolboy-like knowledge of a few theories which are for the most part outdated, are often thought of as ideological work. The Church looks on its faithful in the same way and makes efforts to infuse them with faith and so to save their souls with the sophistry of the apostles.

Ideology is everything, more or less, which originates in society and comes to the mind through man's activities in society. Education, music, literature, radio, film, theater, social and ethical norms, etc. belong in this category. A real ideological struggle would only be one which raises the cultural and scientific level in all spheres of the spiritual life of the society, and one also which to an even greater extent offers the same to the individual without imposing it on him. Neither a theory nor a practice which teaches obsolete roles and warps the living socialist idea into a non-existent "socialist" religion are ideology. All of life in all its forms, in the city and in all parts of the country, is socialism, not any political part of it alone.

The present dull, outmoded, and superimposed bureaucratic methods of ideological activity here remind us of the Soviet Union's. We, however, are not the Soviet Union and our communists are not Stalin's servile officials. There they teach and are taught what Stalin said, what Marx and Lenin preached, but there still exist the shedding of innocent human blood, despotism, famine and backwardness. This ideological activity within the Soviet Union has no connection with either science or life. Its goals are neither science nor life. These methods are excellent for keeping people backward. They resemble anaesthesia of the conscience, because human conscience operates against the profit of shady bosses and masters of despotism.

And would it not be profitable, in this case, to look into history a little, and also to look around ourselves a little more? There are no working-class movements in the world today, except the Stalinist ones, which have the same working methods as our League of Communists. Nonetheless, there are non-Stalinist working-class movements which live and develop in spite of the fact that they have neither police, courts, nor press to support them. Lenin's party had no such working methods as compulsory education led by committees and a professional apparatus, compulsory attendance of basic party organization meetings, but Lenin used a professional apparatus in exceptional circumstances, although he did insist on compulsory meetings of basic organizations as a principle of militant work. These Stalinist party methods and organizational principles ultimately became the forms of an authoritarian apparatus.

Although we can explain and justify why these conditions still exist here, it is not clear why they should continue to do so.

The Essence of the Problem: Yugoslavia is the only country in the world with men and movements claiming to be Leninist. (The Stalinists and Trotskyists clearly are not Leninist.) We have no reason to be ashamed of that. On the contrary. But there is no reason for being that alone. We must be logical to the end if we really want to be socialist.

No one would be more astonished than Vladimir Ilyich if he saw what remained of his works and ideas in his own country. Vladimir Ilyich was not concerned with creating a new ideology (a higher phase of Marxism, as Stalin put it) and least of all with creating permanent and unchanging methods. As he said, the major theme of his teaching was his concept of the state (of the struggle for power and revolution) and in this connection his concept of the party. However, his thought and his methods (the party of a certain type) were adapted to a specific time, which means to the period of preparing for the struggle for power, for annihilation of the bourgeoisie, and for the confiscation of their property.[3]

We built our Leninist party, and later our state, with our own forces but under the influence of Lenin's ideas and Stalin's interpretation of Leninism. Much of our theory and many methods in our practice which we consider unalloyed Marxist products are, in fact, Stalin's heritage. If these theories and practices—with our own very important Yugoslav additions—were once appropriate to our reality, particularly at the time of our revolutionary struggle, they are no longer appropriate today. And this applies not only to our Leninist-Stalinist concepts and methods, but also to pure Leninist ideas (except in the most general forms).[4]

First and foremost, our concepts of our party and our League of Communists most importantly belong to those obsolete methods and ideas. The Communist Party of Yugoslavia was good—such as it was—for preparing for the armed struggle and for the armed struggle itself. If it remains as it is, however, it will retard progress. Its formerly revolutionary methods were forced to change into undemocratic and despotic methods because they do not fit the socialist trends of a socialist society.

No one thinks of opposing the League of Communists. We only oppose the Stalinist remnants inside the League, or to put it more accurately, Stalin's version of the Leninist Party, because it retards progress, particularly democratic progress.

That isn't all. The fundamental question is the work of the basic party organizations and their ideological activity, because they reveal most strongly the old trends as well as the tendencies toward new ones. The Communist Party of Yugoslavia also contained many such trends. If we do not renounce these old methods, we cannot talk about the changes in the major role of the Communist Party of Yugoslavia, and we cannot stress that the League of Communists is different from the CPY, or from Stalin's version of the Leninist Party, because centralized and compulsory ideological activity were the bases of the old CPY (and of every revolutionary party). Some comrades, accustomed to old principles, consider gradual elimination of such principles as liquidation of the League of Communists and as a renunciation of communism and socialism.

The Leninist form of the party and the state has become obsolete (the dictatorship based on the Party), and must always and everywhere become obsolete as soon as revolutionary conditions no longer exist and democracy begins to live.[5] We mean the Leninist form in a most general sense, because the form is variable and can differ from Lenin's according to time and place. Our form of state and party also has differed—sometimes it was more Leninistically centralized and ideologically uniform than Lenin's state and party—in order to express the practical needs of the revolution or the influence of Stalinism, or both.

Our progress can proceed in two directions—toward a Leninist form of state and party which cannot be democratic today, or toward a renunciation of that form for a more democratic, free and decentralized form of political life and struggle. Freer and more flexible forms of political and ideological work are already appearing, if only as tendencies; we have less dogmatism and more democratic and humane relations among comrades and citizens of our country, so we can only delay the dilemma, but we cannot avoid it.

The democratic changes we are discussing will have enormous effects on further development of our domestic social, spiritual and political progress. The logic and the basis of these changes are in economic development and in economic relations. However, obsolete political and spiritual forms are still capable of retarding economic development. Social development and progress means unity of conscious elements with the unorganized masses, a unity of antithetical elements which incessantly accommodate to one another, or put pressure on one another, in order to be more united and bound to each other.

These changes in democracy and in the free struggle of opinion must not provoke profound social repercussions and difficulties in our country. Evolution and reform are creative and revolutionary; they are only possible in our country now, after the Revolution, on the basis of the socialized ownership of industry and commerce, and in a time of developing democracy and strengthening independence.

All our present dominant esthetic, pholisophical and ethical, as well as our political, economic and social theories—particularly the last three—will be shaken, and have already been shaken, by the social changes in everything except fundamentals. Only the basic materialist (Marx's and Marxist) theses and discoveries will persist, but they will persist only if they develop. Otherwise, they will persist as dead truths, dogmas, truths that once were truths and are true no more, because a truth can survive as such only if it progresses.

[1] In the majority of urban centers, this is unnecessary. In rural areas, the transformation may be slower. I emphasize the fact that we are now using the phrase a "course of events"; we speak of "orientations" and no longer of things that must be done overnight. We have reached the stage where we need no longer be precipitate in our decisions.

[2] Of course, these are only the most general ideas for orientation. In theory and practice, which differ according to varying conditions anyway, our politically gifted organizers will find better and more appropriate specific solutions.

[3] This doctrine, which under new conditions should be developed further, was perpetuated by Stalin, who converted it into oaths of loyalty and inflexible rules so that he might transform the party into a privileged class and the state into an element of despotic exploitation. The essence of Stalinism consists of transforming and "strengthening" the revolutionary Leninist party and focusing it as the only force and power for building socialism. (This was Stalin's theory of the transitional character of the party.) And anyway, Stalinism means abandoning both the theory and practice of Leninism.

Even if Lenin's theory and practice had been applied over a longer period, they would eventually have degenerated into despotic methods similar to those used by Stalin. Stalin personified the counterrevolution by killing the revolutionaries and suppressing socialist criticism. He established a bureaucratic despotism in place of the revolutionary democracy of the masses. But even if Stalin had not done that, provided he did not develop the revolution further, into democracy, socialist democracy, he would still have been the personification of stagnation.

[4] No one can diminish the great world-historic importance of the October Revolution, and of Lenin, to the cause of socialism in general and to us in particular. But at best, the October Revolution was only a single step in theoretical and practical progress, and cannot be of exclusive value today. Reality has changed; the Soviet Union has become state capitalist; and monopolist capitalism has turned into state capitalism.

*A detailed and realistic analysis would probably reveal that both as party and masses we were different from Lenin's party and state. We were more democratic to a considerable extent. (For example, we always accepted the principle of personal responsibility.) We did not follow this principle, however, during any particular period. (The intra-party clash of opinion and the atmosphere of spiritual freedom was evidently greater in Lenin's time.) *De facto,* we were ideologically closer to Lenin because we were revolutionaries. In practice, however, we were (frequently) closer to Stalin because we were forced to be by our own bureaucratic reality, as well as by the influence of and inheritance from the USSR.

a The name of the Yugoslav Communist Party was changed to the League of Yugoslav Communists at the Sixth Party Congress held in Zagreb from November 2-5, 1952. The declared purpose of the change was to foster "democratic forms of authority," and to assign to communists as their basic purpose "the political and ideological education of the masses." The League was to act as an organ of persuasion and not as a direct organ of leadership and administration.

b The People's Front changed its name to the Socialist Alliance of the Working People of Yugoslavia at its Fourth Congress, held in Belgrade, February 25, 1953. The declared purpose was to establish a "united and active mass political organization of conscious fighters for socialism." Communists were advised that they were "only a part of the Alliance" and that it was "the basic and main organization through which their political and ideological activity was to be carried out."

The People's Front was established during the war under the name Anti-Fascist People's Front of National Liberation. It included members of non-communist parties who had joined the Partisans. The Front was under Communist Party leadership, and remained so.

ANATOMY OF A MORAL

No one, least of all this young woman, could have guessed that life could suddenly become so bleak, in the very midst of what seemed to the mass of people to be so pure, so spiritual, so free of the petty, vulgar and intruding meanness and greed which naturally spring from privation and backwardness, and which she had painfully fought against all through her childhood and youth until those singing, shining summer days when she was married. But, to her, they were grim and distressing days.

She was a twenty-one-year-old opera singer and aware of her beauty, but that did not make her proud, not even in her own heart. She was conscious of her strong, slender body; she rejoiced in it as one rejoices in something one has but which does not really belong to one. She was without particular or strongly marked bents or passions. She delighted in everything and sorrow was a stranger to her, at least until she met that profound and incurable sorrow which only disillusionment can bring.

Her only irresistible love was music. She devoted her entire being to it, not only in a special, intellectual way, but in the unusually passionate manner so characteristic of musically-educated people with an exceptionally fine ear. This insatiable passion burned in every nerve and fiber, and fired her imagination; it had sent her to conservatories for training and finally had brought her to the stage. Because she came from a large and poor family, after her marriage she still retained a conspicuous and somewhat vulgar thriftiness, a spiritual naivete, a directness and humility. Had her husband been less quick in reacting to everything, particularly where personal considerations were involved, she might have had no troubles and sorrows except those which life brings to everyone, even to the comfortable and the carefree.

Although her husband's haughty way of treating her in front of others as if she were an inexperienced girl (which she actually was, in spite of the theatrical surroundings in which she lived and worked, not so much to earn a living, but because she loved music and singing) annoyed her, this strong and mature man's patronizing air pleased her when displayed in private. She felt as if she had never lost her old, warm though poor little nest, but had merely exchanged it for another, perhaps more solid and enduring.

Thus, she was typical of thousands of young, beautiful women who were growing up and marrying year after year in this young and beautiful country. She lived like other women, with her small worries and her large dreams. What simple people might have considered unusual and extraordinary was her vocation of opera singer and also that she was the wife of a high official, but in her naivete she didn't think this extraordinary in modern times and in a socialist country.

Not only did she have a presentiment, but she knew in advance, that many women would envy her good marriage. Her husband was a high official; he was handsome, virile, and strong; above all, he was a famous wartime commander, which always appeals to women's vivid imaginations and evokes their envy: it makes them think of lost opportunities. As soon as peace was established, this man who had spent his youth in wars and in prisons wanted to have a good time and to amuse himself, regardless of Party or other restrictions, deaf to whatever remorse he might feel for his transgressions. She knew all this from his casual comments, and his frivolous nature told her much more. Although she was imbued with very strong, even harsh, moral precepts, drilled into her from birth, she was a modern girl who knew perfectly well that she couldn't change life, morality or marriage in advance, but she *was* prepared to struggle to alter and redirect them afterwards. So she accepted her husband's past calmly and sincerely, with that inner cheerful ease which people have when they acknowledge something which has been and cannot be undone but which, after all, is not so terrible since it will never return.

She anticipated, therefore, that the women with whom her husband had been intimate, as well as those who had failed to share his bachelor adventures but knew about them, would soon turn up with their petty intrigues, phone calls, anonymous letters and the like, problems which might frighten an old-fashioned woman, but which to her were simple. They didn't impress her or, for that matter, her contemporaries.

She was also cheered by the thought that if she entered this new, clean and spiritual milieu with her husband, as the wife of a high official among the wives of other high officials, all of whom seemed simple and unpretentious, these annoyances would soon become insignificant details, petty, loose-tongued maliciousness, and then, after a while, would stop altogether, once the world realized how solidly grounded and strong their marriage was.

And indeed that was the way it happened. The mean and malicious annoyances, the clandestine phone calls to her husband, the dirty stories told in sordid detail, the spiteful and bitter anonymous letters, became less and less frequent from day to day, from week to week. But contrary to her expectations, her new milieu not only failed to show her affection, but refused altogether to accept her. She faced a massive, icy and impenetrable wall which no one had warned her she would meet. She was the last to realize it. With her postwar ideas, as a new Party member and as a young wife, though she was anxious and bewildered by all the new, strange events of married life, she still swooned in the rosy glow and flame of her first love and happiness. . . .

Matrimony has been and always will be, whatever the social order and its outward forms, one of the basic units and foundations of social life. It is one of the generally recognized achievements of civilized life, a value which belongs to no single class of society, but is the result of a long, continuous process of humanization of social relations, an institution without which society would regress and turn savage. Hence, it has always been a generally accepted rule and duty for man to help young married couples to establish as natural and warm relations between themselves as is possible. It is an ancient custom, even among peoples of the most primitive cultures, for relatives, friends, acquaintances, or even casual guests, all to show—by celebration, by giving gifts, and other kindnesses and courtesies—that they wish to help to pro-

mote the best possible relations and understanding between the new partners, to help unite what, at best, is
difficult to harmonize, and not to make life more difficult
for the new couple.

This is especially true where bride and groom come
from entirely different milieus, with conflicting ideas and
habits, and therefore react differently to the new situation.
These are unwritten codes but they express a multitude
of the society's conscious and spontaneous aspirations in
its long and devious march toward a better society. There
are deviations from these rules, but not by society as such,
or by entire classes of society. Those who do deviate are
the endless procession of human individuals, or groups
of individuals, whom an unfortunate social order has
forced into selfishness and greed as a means of survival,
even at the price of the suffering of others. Courtesy,
tenderness of heart and good manners have, in the course
of time, become the unwritten hall-mark of the humane
individual and of society as a whole.

Our young woman did not, of course, know all this,
nor could she have expressed herself even if she had.
But deep in her heart she was aware of it, as all other
individuals are, too.

This young woman was hurt, therefore, unhappy
both as woman and wife, when this new, highly idealized
milieu, or the greatest and decisive part of it, greeted
her and her marriage with contempt and hatred. They displayed the hatred with an intensity and obstinacy strange
by any accepted social standards, and inexplicable unless
one admits that there exists an animal craving for main-
taining acquired social status, a bestial urge more stupid,
savage and monstrous, more merciless than any fight
among wild animals. Look at what happened! By the

simple appearance of a young woman, the social position of that clique was suddenly, fatefully and incomprehensibly menaced merely because she was one of those unknown and undeserving women who not only had not been in the war, but who could not become an ordinary member of a basic Party unit, or of a students' Party committee, and who, to top it all off, was—hear this!—an actress, an actress, mind you, like all the rest of them who, goodness knows how, managed to "worm" themselves into the Party which now—good heavens!—includes all sorts of rabble. This is the way that clique indignantly reacted.

True, one must admit there was a difference, though slight, between the men's behavior and that of their wives. The men were, or pretended to be, indifferent to the newcomer in their hallowed and secluded class which, when not loafing in its magnificent parvenu offices, moved from place to place, lived in its own select and restricted summer resorts, gathered in its own exclusive clubs, slept in its own secluded houses, sat in its own exclusive theaters and stadium boxes. Their wives, however, were more direct. They regarded the new marriage not only with profound aversion and disapproval, but they met it with open hatred, showing thereby that they had suddenly promoted themselves to be the watchdogs of an imaginary—their own—moral code, established to answer their instantaneous urge to protect a class closed off in various high official posts and made inaccessible to anyone from a lower class.

Well, these virtuous ladies, themselves wives and mothers, who sermonized in public about women and equality, and some of whom had been leaders of the feminist movement in times past, had never before remonstrated with a husband for having married "someone who had nothing in common with us"; that is, women of a special stratum and a particular kind of job. In this case, however, their blind bias would stop at nothing, not even the fact that the young bride's husband was almost twice her age and in every way much more mature than she was. Moreover, he was a veteran communist whose faults, even if judged by the moral standards of that particularly isolated set, should have merited a much more severe reproof. But . . . well . . . "she never had any connections with us"; meaning by that "us" themselves and communism, the people and society at large. In brief, she was an intruder, an outcast, and there was no place for "her" among "them."

The groom's past offenses were dismissed lightly. The worst that happened was that he would be casually or jokingly reminded that he "was getting a little old" and that—forgive my frankness—"no wonder the meat of young chickens suited him better. . . ." It was his bride who had to bear the brunt and was made the scapegoat. She had to take all the blame, often expressed in the most frivolous and insulting allusions. It was she who "had caught him on the hip, the poor old guy," or "the poor old warrior couldn't hold off the last offensive," or "the wars have worn our dear Comrade out and a lifted skirt was enough. . . ."

It was consistent with these women and their way of life that they did not turn their knives against him. At the end of the war, many of them had been soldiers and were dispersed into offices, Party committees and ministerial cabinets. They had all looked longingly at the famous, brilliant and handsome war commander every time they saw him pass. Even now, though they were all married, they still felt sorry for their respected comrade who had, in the end, "sunk" so low and permitted himself to be "caught," "hooked," and "trapped." But this was not the main motive for their actions. They had another motive, more real and intense. What mattered to them was that he belonged to their set. No doubt about that. He had kept all his former rank and functions because of his ability, his talent, and his political reliability. So, he really "belonged to them." For "them," he was not an upstart or intruder who had crashed "among them" into this "communism of theirs."

No one bothered to ask himself, nor could they all in their exclusiveness ask, who the bride really was, where she'd come from, who her parents, brothers and sisters were. The only important factor for this set was that she belonged to a different social stratum, that she had "illegally" sneaked into the group of people who had fought in the war, won the power we now wield and the freedom we now enjoy, and who, now that the war is over, all occupy ranking positions in the state, have automobiles, travel by pullman, get their food and clothing at special stores, spend their holidays in secluded villas, summer resorts and spas, and who, on the basis of all this, have gradually convinced themselves that they are exceptionally meritorious and that all of this privilege is so very natural and logical that only fools and obdurate enemies could have any doubts about it.

In such circumstances, their secluded life and psychological experience have given rise to ideas and notions not only typical of this select milieu, but revealing a pretension to absolutism; that is, thought of as binding and permanent for everyone. Permanent is perhaps not the proper term, because the dialectics taught in the

higher Party schools and institutes do not accept perma-
nence as a concept. At any rate, these notions were
considered by this caste to typify communism, socialism
and true humanity.

It was, therefore, a foregone conclusion that the wife
of a high-ranking official, such as our bridegroom was
and would continue to be for a considerable time to
come, could only be an individual with the lustre of certain quite definite Party qualities, and of course, with a
similar past. An "ordinary" woman was out of the question, at least as his wedded wife.

Moreover, since real ownership no longer exists in
this country, at least not in the cities, except in the sense
of bonuses and all sorts of privileges derived from official
positions, there could be no dowry either. Beauty, spiritual qualities, physical attraction have never been regarded as a proper dowry in a society which counts on
the dowry if there is any; generally, beauty is considered a matter of taste, something one may be inclined
to personally and emotionally, but it is never among the
hard, tangible things that comprise a dowry. Consequently, the dowry for a good match in the new conditions in our country can be either another high official
position, corresponding to that occupied by the groom if
he happens to be an official, or other equally acceptable
merits of the bride. The official rank of the bride can, of
course, be lower, because she is a woman. As a rule, and
quite regardless of spiritual affinities or physical attrac-
tions, love is demeaned and enslaved by this new type
of dowry.

Our bride had beauty. She also loved. But these
were nothing. She did not bring with her the new type
of dowry which would have gilded everything. She was,

153

therefore, without merit to the new regime. She was a simple, ordinary woman, only an actress. That was her sole uniqueness, but it was also the basic, brutal motive and excuse for the insidious hatred, scorn and icy ostracism she faced, the more incomprehensible and dreadful because it was spontaneous and taciturn.

The young couple was received with hostility by those very people who looked on themselves as the most qualified—in fact, solely qualified—to watch and ward and buttress the holiness of marriage, and of whom it could be said that their own marriages were more or less successful. In this case, however, the general rule that marriage is a sacred thing was frivolously overruled and despised the moment it clashed with their raging instinctive interests, at the bottom of which lurked the still-hidden but already irresistible solidarity of the caste. The frivolous ease with which in this case sacred principles, as soon as they disagreed with caste interests, were trampled down and forgotten, unmasked the frightful hypocrisy of these morals and of the majority of these respected wives, all of whom boasted—and perhaps they are convinced—that theirs were real love matches. Perhaps theirs were. Love is not something one can separate from society, something purely emotional, but it is the sentimental expression of an endless series of influences, ideas, customs, traditions, psychological and physical desires, condensed into one feeling, into a single experience. In this case, however, they denied love and the right to love to anyone not a member of their own secluded circle, particularly where the love was of one of their caste for an outsider. Call it whatever you like, but not love!

The personal right to a free life with all its mistakes and failings is thus destroyed, and the interest in personal fate and misfortune, in man's destiny, vanishes as soon as it encounters the dried-out and unyielding spirit of the caste, the more stubborn and difficult because it is so recently created.

Such was the mentality of this one of the higher social circles. It grew somewhat unawares from a quite natural and normal logic and necessity; namely, that favorable conditions should be afforded leaders so that they can work and live. This attitude and system proliferated in all directions, from top to bottom, everywhere. Thus, people were classified into categories and strata, near-strata, kindred categories or professions, etc., each neatly placed in secluded pigeonholes but bound together by a common solidarity which was not so much the product of ideological or moral unity as the product of the same way of life, of similar interests arising from the nature of the official authority they wielded and the manner in which they had acquired that authority.

On the lower, inferior social strata, life was franker; more brutal, savage and crude. A district secretary's new wife, for example, overnight becomes the first lady of the district irrespective of her intellectual and other adornments. She chooses her friends carefully and everyone regards it as a privilege to join her exalted set.

Friendships between husbands and between wives were made and unmade according to the political changes within the circle, and according to how one either climbed to higher positions or slipped down to lower ones on the ladder of hierarchy. But in one respect, every circle remained closed and impenetrable: in the common determination to keep out of the Holy of Holies any "unworthy" newcomer, or anyone not of the same, or close to the same, level of political importance.

Endless secret tragedies inevitably followed one another.

The young woman suffered all this from the very beginning.

On the very day of her wedding she was standing with her husband and their best man, a lively, brisk and haughty young general, on the terrace at the entrance to the state box of the new football stadium. She had no idea about the box or who had the "right" to sit in it. She didn't even know that they would take her to that box. She had been invited and gone along with them after their wedding luncheon, and so now she was in their company. It was a glorious but cool afternoon in early summer and she was very happy, feeling airy and buoyant, though a little sad that she was leaving her girlhood behind. The crowd was slow, sluggish in its movement into the arena, which looked like a great stone bee-hive. As so often before in her life, when experiencing something fresh and beautiful, especially when facing large, lively and congenial crowds, she had an innermost feeling that people were good, in spite of their petty selfishness or malice, and the reason they did wicked things to one another (so she thought) was merely because they were bored or because misfortunes with which they could not cope assailed them.

While she was looking down at the crowd, sincerely believing them one huge, gay and good entity, she suddenly saw a slender young woman walk over and begin to talk to her husband. This lady was unobtrusively elegant and visibly cheerful. Looking at her pleased the bride. She didn't know the lady, though she had seen her in the street and had also seen her picture. She had heard nice things about her intelligence and simplicity, and had also heard that she was the wife of a tenacious, clever high economic official who was very popular with the people and with the students among whom she had moved prior to her marriage. As he was said to be a very humane, just and modest man, full of sincere understanding for human misfortunes, so was she, his wife, famed as a cheerful, pleasant, intelligent and simple woman.

At the moment, the bride was not particularly eager to make her acquaintance, though she felt it would be pleasant to talk to her now when, eyes wide open and eager for new impressions, she was entering a new life. But since no one thought to introduce them, or thought it necessary to do so, she preferred not to look directly at this lovely woman. When she heard a harsh, grating sound in her husband's voice, she turned in their direction. His eyes were snapping, always a sign that he was angry, while the lady smiled ironically at him and said something, threw the young bride a quick expressionless glance, as if looking at something dead, broken and useless, and then hurried after her husband.

The bride felt that something had happened.

Who was this woman? What was she to her new husband, her bridegroom? It never occurred to her that this lady could have been one of those who had phoned, as, in fact, she was not. But what had happened? She looked at her husband again as if wanting to ask a question, but felt no definite response. He smiled back, put his arm around her waist, and drew her near him, lightly so that no one else could notice it, yet firmly enough for her to feel it and understand. That, too, was one of his gestures. Then, she also smiled as if nothing had happened and acknowledged his pressure with a dream-like touch. Perhaps it wasn't even a touch, only the breath of her body against his chest.

But something really had happened.

Later, the young woman learned that the following conversation had taken place between her groom and the lady. She: "Is that your beauty?" He: "Yes. How do you like her?" She: "Well, it depends. Judging by her looks, she's all right . . . but it seems she didn't see much of the war." He: "How could she? She wasn't even thirteen then." She: "I know, I know. It couldn't have been too hard for you to find her. She found you. Only I can't understand why you married her. There are so many others around, good old comrades with so much . . ." He: ". . . I married her because I love her, and not . . ." She: "Yes, yes, sure. . . . Love, love! Love burns like a wet blanket would burn in the Sava River. Weren't you a bit hasty, attracted by her youth and beauty?" He: "Well, a man marries a woman and not the forum of public opinion. . . ."

With her husband's arm around her, the bride entered the box and since all the foregoing had happened by pure coincidence, she'd forgotten it by the time she was passing between chairs to her seat. Other impressions overwhelmed her. The unpleasant encounter was easily forgotten in the thrilling beauty and motley of the over-crowded arena. Waves of applause surged and swelled, now here, now there, depending on where the beloved champion team was playing and running on the field. Now, the first encounter with the other women in the box could not be avoided. It was a shock for the young woman. While the players, waiting for the umpire, were stretching or warming up, her husband's friend, his best man, introduced her to some of his comrades and the four wives who were there in the box, and also to the lady she had seen at the entrance and about whom her curiosity had been aroused. Polite and smiling, the men shook hands with her but a moment later forgot all about her, involved with the spectacle down on the field. The women extended their hands reluctantly, askance. Their handshakes were limp, without pressure, and wordless. Then, with obvious intent they turned their heads away, so overtly that she could scarcely help noticing it. The woman she had met at the entrance—the most elegant and intelligent of the lot—did not even shake hands with her. She made only a casual bow and remarked in a joking, reproachful and icy voice, "You're an actress, aren't you? Is that so? Yes, they told me you were an actress. The other actresses who married our generals never come here."

What did all that mean, those stiff, cold greetings and those words, the young bride asked herself.

A wall suddenly appeared, a wall which dozens of strong hands had abruptly put up criss-cross in the box between her and the others, even between her and her husband, who was looking the other way and was, to all appearances, passionately following the game.

The bride saw nothing of the game. Her favorite team was playing and like all the other young people there in the stands, among whom she had grown up, she wanted to shout with enthusiasm, encourage, yell her disapproval when a play was unfair, but she couldn't. She couldn't move a muscle and she couldn't think. No, she couldn't do it, not only because it would be strange, unusual and incomprehensible in that exalted box filled with people all too busy with affairs of state to pay attention to such childish effusions, but because those glacial encounters and the thick ice around her, impenetrable and incomprehensible, made her feel frozen stiff down to hitherto unknown depths, so cold and stone-hard that everything in her still seemed to be in the same place— her thoughts, wishes, feelings, everything—but at a standstill, paralyzed. She felt the cold gaze of many eyes staring at her from the left, the right, and from behind her, as if she were some curiosity hurled into their midst from a faraway and unknown darkness. She felt those eyes were hard, tangible, pointed things pressing lightly but unyielding against her, giving her an icy sensation. She turned around once or twice, as if she would like to run away. Immediately, those staring, piercing eyes would turn away from her. These women didn't want to be caught; they didn't even want to show her that she, the young girl and newcomer, could have aroused anything more than mere unpleasant bewilderment.

Never afterwards was the young woman able to explain how it happened that, during the intermission, she stepped over to the woman whom she had met at the entrance. Perhaps she did it because she was so confused and forlorn. Perhaps an unsuspected, dormant sense of human dignity awoke in her. Perhaps she wanted to say something nice, something that would remove the wall between her and this apparently so subtle, so well-educated and refined woman, who by her sustained efforts and studies had risen from a semi-peasant, petty-bourgeois Serbian milieu, then managed to refine her husband —at least to some extent—and finally, through hard work, the grim hardships of war and tenacious service in the Party apparatus, had lifted herself to the high level of a politically and culturally well-educated woman. The young bride approached her, but didn't know what to say. "I am," the bride began, and wondered why she should be stuttering. ". . . I am not what you think actresses are. Some of them, perhaps, are that kind. But I . . ."

The other cut in, "I'm not saying that. But your profession is one which. . . . After all, why should I explain to you and . . . make you feel uncomfortable? One thing I should like to make clear to you, however, and I tell you this with the best of goodwill and for your own sake: you'll never be acceptable company for our comrades and women comrades." Then she turned around softly and left. The bride had no time to say anything. Subsequently, she was sorry that she had had no time to say at least one thing, specifically, that she would never beg for their friendship. She sat down, broken and lonely.

She wanted to leave. She heard strange noises in her head, not those from the arena, but her own, internal noises like the rapid throbbing of drums. . . . In her despair she looked at her husband and down at the field. They were all enjoying themselves, and no one paid any attention to her. She then heard one of the women remark, "You told her off properly, and well done." A quiet, approving murmur greeted her words. . . .

Maybe she should run away now? Where? And how? Should she cry and make a scandal for her husband? No, not here in public would she weep and not today, on her wedding day. And he, her husband, suspected nothing of the drama. She wanted to scream but was too numb and weak and confused even for that. She felt as if she were shrinking, growing smaller, and oh, how cold she felt, and how slowly her frightened heart was beating.

Only when she was alone with her husband that evening did she begin to cry bitterly and despairingly.

That was their first free evening, entirely their own, in her husband's apartment, and it was their wedding night, the beginning of a new life for her, in a different home and in new, quite strange surroundings. At first, the young woman implored her husband not to abandon her. A moment afterward, she entreated him to let her go for his own sake, pleaded that he should not cut himself off from his friends and his former life because of her. She swore that she would leave the theater the next day, then began to cry because she might be called upon to do the only thing it was impossible for her to do, because her entire life, body and soul, was music and melody, and she could never resist her inner urge to sing, to sing those ever-flowing tunes. Her abandonment to music was now so total and incurable that she knew her body would ring with unknown songs even after she was dead.

But this was only the beginning of this disastrous love match.

Since in this particular milieu, character and personal worth are rated by the rank an individual occupies in the hierarchy, and above all, by the actual power a person wields—both consequences of the Revolution—the women of these secluded circles are slowly losing their personal qualities, their personal values and their individuality, so that gradually they are no longer judged by their individual worth but only by the jobs their husbands hold. The line of behavior taken by the lady the bride had met at the stadium entrance soon spread, therefore, and became the general rule of conduct for all. This was not so much because *she* had acted as an individual, but because her husband was important and wielded great power. It didn't matter that he was entirely uninterested in the quarrel and that he himself was well-disposed toward the couple; his position gave enough weight to the line his wife took to make it general and binding in the exclusive circle.

Actually, this lady was one of the best of the lot, one of the more cultured, humane and moral ones, yet she supported and gave finality to the stupid, rash stand against anyone who, perchance, wanted to enter that exalted circle—because the circle imagined itself to be exalted and thereby made itself exalted—in which illusions whirled and phantoms of the past caroused. This is but another confirmation of the old and unchanged truth that people are not what they imagine themselves to be, but what the conditions in which they live have made them. They are what a specific social order, for which they stand, has made them.

Now, to return to this woman (the one the bride had met at the entrance), let us say this. She was the product of partly traditional (religious and petty-bourgeois), partly acquired (dogmatic and bureaucratic) morals. What had she done? She had bowed to the accepted morals without question. She had become a willing instrument in the hands of the exclusive set's self-made relations, relations which had already become actuality. However, and this is rare, she maintained the external forms of civilized behavior. But this did not change the essential facts of the situation or still less cause her any qualms; she did not stop to think that one should have some consideration for and show good

163

will toward those who, less fortunate, have no hierarchical rank and no deserved merits for joining that higher circle. Yes, we know of such qualms. They occurred at the time of the struggle with the Cominform, but they simply followed the rising tide of the democratic spirit. As soon as the tide subsided for a while, the old caste mentality was reawakened in new form, abstract, unreal and absurd in the face of the way privilege was crumbling under the impact of the country's improving living conditions. Conditions did change for the better and with them the general human approach also changed.

This woman was quite capable of understanding all this much more rapidly and better than many of the others. She must also have understood very well the inevitability of these changes. But her dogmatic, traditional and Party moral code—once revolutionary—was too unyielding and, therefore, ugly. These morals had taken root in her personality during a joyless youth of difficult struggles and many personal sacrifices. She herself had had difficulties in breaking through the gate and in penetrating into the higher circle. She had only been a personnel manager in the institution run by her future husband who was, at that time, still an obdurate bachelor. When she married him, she was strongly opposed by the very same exclusive circle, already formed before she had knocked at its doors. But this was now forgotten because she was a fighter—she had been a soldier—and had fought for her place in the circle. This other girl, of course, was made of different stuff; she was only an actress, a singer, or, as she was disdainfully referred to, a "thrush."

This, then, is the so-called logic of hierarchy: get

on top and then keep out the "unworthy," the "immoral" ones. This, then, is the horrible logic of so-called reality, of the rulers and the privileged, which has made selfish monsters of heroic men and women.

Just think: all these exalted women came from semi-peasant surroundings and were semi-educated. Some have not changed and have remained simple, particularly those politically and morally educated before the war. Unfortunately, these are few and are always looked down upon by the others as hypocrites and conservatives. Suddenly, the majority of them began to develop complexes, not only toward the outer world but also toward themselves, to develop a rigid aristocratic style and to assume a manner to match their illusions. They then began a race among themselves to see which ones could outclimb the others, push themselves forward, each quoting her own unsuspected wartime and other achievements while running down those of others. The next move was to identify their own persons and "rights" with those functions and rights which belonged to their husbands. Many went even further than that. Some of them—and this is by far the most ridiculous and ugly aspect of the matter—began to grab and hoard de-luxe furniture and works of art, tasteless of course, but by means of which they satisfied their primitive instincts of greed and imagined and puffed-up notions of their social status, with all the pretentious omniscience of the ignorant.

This type of woman—not the same category as that woman the bride had met at the stadium entrance—unfortunately outnumbered the others, and was much coarser, much more direct and uncouth. Most conspicuous in their rudeness were those very women who had no grounds whatever for pride in having practiced in their youth the virtues which they now demanded of others and of the young bride.

Let me quote. One of them, paraphrasing penny-trash literature, said, "I always smell a repulsive odor of decay whenever I'm in the same room with her." This woman is famous because she was young at the time when girl members of SKOJ [the Communist Youth Organization] thought that liberation from petty-bourgeois prejudices such as virginity and marital fidelity were the first requisites for emancipation of women. Another complained, "One can no longer recognize women comrades. One doesn't know who is a comrade and who is a whore." Another is quoted as having said, "By her profession alone, she can be nothing but a whore." This last opinion was the one most widely accepted.

One evening the young bride went to the home of a friend with her husband. The hostess, sitting in an armchair, greeted her by offering a cold hand, passing it negligently over her shoulder, and did not speak a single word to her during the entire evening. It was, by the way, common knowledge that the hostess could not boast of a very virtuous life before her marriage. Now she felt the need to show off her culture and elegance. She had learned English and taken piano lessons, and there, in her own house, she dared to accuse the young bride of things the bride had never done. The husband got up hurriedly, took his young wife by the hand, and left without saying a single word. It was indeed a horrible evening.

Wherever they went together, they were confronted with the same icy ostracism, which she had done nothing to provoke. In a restaurant, if she sat down at a table already occupied by another woman from this clique, a third would soon turn up and motion the second away with signs and gestures. Everywhere it was the same. . . .

Since the husband of the young bride neither wanted to, nor could, tear himself entirely away from his milieu, it was inevitable that a wider and wider gulf of estrangement should open between them. This virile, healthy and tough man, feeling the strain of the situation, began to be shaken by internal conflicts which constantly demanded: How on earth is all this possible? Where does it all come from? And why? Is it possible among people like these? Are these the new ethics? Is this communism? Is this socialism?

With a womanly gentleness uniquely her own, the young wife began to avoid social engagements in order to spare her husband awkward situations where he would again be snubbed, ostracized and consequently become angry afterwards. Slowly, almost imperceptibly, they developed the custom of his going out by himself while she stayed at home alone.

But because she was a human being after all, young and talented, and had her own profession, she could not live isolated from everybody. Thus, gradually, she turned for friendships to her own world of the stage, although previously she had disliked the theatrical world almost as much as she liked music, rhythm and song.

While she was a young communist girl still in school, she often dreamed of how she would endeavor to bring new morals, new creative élan, and new relationships into the theatrical world. For now, under socialism, this was quite feasible. Nowadays, the path to the stage no longer passed through princely alcoves and bankers' bedrooms. Her marriage to a good and prominent man only strengthened those ideals.

Real life, however, proved to be different. The old theatrical world, corroded by intrigue, infected by careerism, and in general corrupted by the Occupation, was used to the facile and frivolous entertainment linked with such a mentality and with such a way of life. Slowly, however, the theater began to link itself to the new regime, since it was a fact of life which could not be avoided —"Theater is theater," they said—although sometimes the actors clashed with the regime both as individuals and as groups. At that time everything seemed to indicate that it was possible to submit to and get along with the new regime. But this accomodation did not by any means signify that the theatrical world had undergone a radical internal and structural change. After her marriage, the young actress began to believe in the stale, fundamental immutability of the theater and its world; the more so because she saw that the other world—which she had childishly believed in and trusted, and which had rejected her—obviously had not dissociated itself from the old world either.

And so the young woman suddenly found herself —as a woman, wife, personality and actress—assailed from all sides and torn between her wishes and the impossibility of achieving them, between her dreams and the bitter realities of life. No wonder that, slowly, she was drawn by unsuspected, profound, and buried urges to return to the old Bohemian, artistic way of life which, from time to time, might offer her transitory joys and oblivion for her grief. With the invisible force of a gathering avalanche, life itself was pushing her towards what one of the women in the exalted set had foretold:

"Sooner or later, she will go down like the others. She belongs to that class." Nonetheless, the young woman kept struggling, resisting for her own sake, for the sake of her conscience and her love. But those people of the caste who boasted that they were apostles of the new had actually long ceased to be that, and therefore, by their stupid, incomprehensible behavior, had clearly pushed the actress back into that world which she could not and would not give up, but which she had wanted to elevate and reform.

Therein lies the moral hypocrisy and inconsistency of the caste people. On the one hand, they condemned and rejected her because, they said, she was an actress. On the other hand, they forced her to be one, and one of the lowest type of actresses, according to their own generally accepted standards. And should it happen some day that, like many others, she also "falls," she would be ostracized and despised—this time with good reason— and serve as a case in point, as has been true of many a good bourgeois wife, that "no honest woman can belong to the theatrical, that is, the lower world, and, to say the least, none of 'ours' could ever come from there. . . ."

In the course of her painful life, pressed as she was on all sides and tormented by inner crises, she came to meet and to know other officially despised women. Some had been trampled down and forgotten, though they were first-class fighters—and what fighters!—in the war. Only now the brutal social reality burst open before her eyes in all its horrifying depth and scope. Only now could she see clearly that neither her profession nor her casual immoralities had provoked this stubborn opposition which knew neither bounds nor pity. No, what they had said were shallow pretexts. The truth was—

she could see it clearly now—that she was considered unworthy of that self-anointed circle which craved pre-eminence and exclusiveness. In that lay the spuriousness of their motives; in that lay the hypocrisy of their morals. Now she knew she could never be, and had no right to be "one of us." And therein also lay the truth.

In the eyes of these people and in consonance with their secluded life, the "one of us" type soon became the only type that really counted. An old truth was once more confirmed. The more people dissociate themselves from the objective reality around them, from society and from life and its problems, the more their own small world begins to appear to them the only real world. Their own interests, concepts of life, moral codes, as they become increasingly abstract, are increasingly identified with the interests of society as a whole, with its absolute truths, its absolute moral codes. The old Aristotelian "eternal" truth which states that it is unnecessary to invent many moral laws, since they can be picked up from the facts of life itself as we go along, put into formulas and fought for, has long since been forgotten in these secluded circles. They have also lost sight of another Aristotelian truth, that one of the foremost duties of politicians is to study the human soul first, particularly its ethics.

Morals and ethics should not be understood to concern sexual norms alone. These latter cover only a very small area of human relationships which grow from and change with the forms of society in which human beings live and move. To reduce ethics and morals to sexual relations alone would be to ignore reality and the whole complex of social relations. The moral values

170

governing sexual life have always been understood in terms of typical, and therefore more humane, personal and social (matrimonial) relations between men and women, and people in general. Among these values, immorality is something exceptional, asocial or anti-social, irrespective of its origins or its causes, whether it lies in the individual or in the given social order.

In the old days, the effort to maintain a sexual morality of restraint and purity was a condition for the internal consolidation of our revolutionary cadres. It was a necessary condition if we wanted to turn out men capable of forgetting their personal interests for the sake of a common cause, and it was necessary to shape characters capable of sacrificing themselves to see fulfillment of their own ambitions in the achievement of the common good. In the course of time, however, with the gradual closing of the circles, whether those above or below, the struggle for purity of sexual relations slowly changed in this secluded milieu—which was, moreover, degenerating under the impact of decadent bureaucratism—into the most vulgar sexual perversions, sexual anarchy, or crude, evil asceticism.

This particular, often much too moral, milieu had great difficulties in understanding these things in other than dogmatic or semi-religious terms. Some individuals never did. But in the old days ours was a real morality, a factual and functional morality, while everywhere around us there reigned total blindness and indifference to any ethical conduct whatsoever, whether with respect to general social relations, or to more humane relations between individuals.

What mattered to this exalted set, however, were

details such as, for example, a presumed immoral act by an actress, while the total destruction of, or contempt for, a human being was of secondary importance. With growing bureaucratism and all it implied, a dogmatism developed which corroded all the ethical values behind which the secluded circles were sheltered and by which they swore. Thus, in the name of marital fidelity, marriages went to pieces; in the name of love, hatred was preached: in the name of human dignity, man was despised; in the name of the new "social order," living people were abused as if they were some remote or abstract beings.

All this appeared in telescoped form in the case of the young actress. We all know that misfortune rarely stops halfway. In the case of the young actress, too, things had to proceed to the bitter end before there was revealed the monstrosity and inhumanity of these exclusive morals, instituted chaotically by impulse, by the mere fact of a secluded way of life and by the bureaucratic methods practiced by the upper caste. All this was done in the name of sublime moral laws and in the name of humanity.

In the first month of her marriage the young wife became pregnant. This secluded set was always enthusiastic about motherhood and babies, provided that these were their own. Many women in that circle were heads of humanitarian, children's, maternity, and similar institutions and organizations. Many of them could scarcely be reproached with not having been active in that kind of work, nor with having been irresponsible and careless.

What was their attitude now toward the young actress? Didn't she belong to a different world from theirs?

Didn't most of them believe and say that by her very profession she was "predestined to be a whore"?

Quick as lightning, the news spread that the actress was pregnant. Unkind and unjust comments followed in its wake. . . . "Ah, that poor child! That's the limit! So quickly!" They did not dare, however, to say openly that the child was not her husband's because that would have been inconsistent with their moral code and thus unnatural. Besides, it would harm the good name of someone who, after all, *did* belong to their set. But then it went on: "Now everything is clear. She caught our dear comrade by playing on his human weaknesses" (upon which, as a rule, they frowned). "He 'made' the child before the marriage and then the poor boy had no other alternative." Intrigue and gossip are quite natural to the way of life of closed groups. Ours was no exception to the rule for it was decaying from within. Periodic reactions, when scandals became too frequent and began to disturb the moral peace of the exalted, or menaced their internal unity and harmony, produced some good effects, but they were short-lived because the structure of the caste's way of life never changed, or at least changed very slowly. The flood of their intrigues burst out spontaneously, it is true, but always started from some factual occurrence. Calumnies were particularly cutting and pitiless whenever an unhallowed, would-be intruder was involved.

Is it possible, it was said, that "one of ours" could fall in love with such a woman? Did you ever hear of such a thing? Since they all agreed that this was impossible, he had been trapped and had to be held. The child was planted on him intentionally, to tie him down forever. So he had no other choice but to marry her, poor boy. What a stupid thing to do! Why didn't he drop her? Why doesn't he do it now? Why give her a chance to use the baby to lead him around by the nose?

None of them stopped to ask whether this was true or not. For them, it was "logical." They had lost all sense of logic because they had lost all connection with real life. Thus, even motherhood was assailed, besmirched, profaned, and turned into a disgusting commercial and careerist transaction.

Although the young actress was inwardly happy, seeing the shape of her body rounding and her girlish, maternal feelings begin to grow into something real and enduring, these sacred feelings met with derision and hatred wherever she went. Did this secluded set think her profession, origin and humble past incompatible with motherhood? "Could such a woman ever be a mother?" they asked. "It's all a fake, isn't it?"

How this story ends is not important, nor what the ultimate fate of the major character in it turns out to be. The factual circumstances which our heroine had to live through in order to survive and take root in that immense, heartless desert of loneliness are also not important. What is important, however, is her fight for the unwritten, imperishable human rights, among them the rights of motherhood.

One evening at the beginning of the theatrical season, at a premiere, she stood there on the stage, embraced by the golden sheaves of light from the spots. Her role in the play was minor but quite long. She played the part of a cheerful, frolicsome chambermaid to a princess of whose amours she knew and whose intrigues she could guess. A typical Renaissance motif in

modern opera. As she was about to finish her gay, popular song, she felt some strange movements of the child
inside her. The theater was jammed. In the boxes of
the first gallery, she saw in the semi-darkness the first-
night audience, among whom she had no difficulty in
recognizing many of the "circle," so many that the
theater seemed filled only with them. They hated her
to the death. They despised her and would trample her
underfoot, the same women who were profoundly moved
by the fate and songs of a Marguerite or a Madame
Butterfly. Yet, they surrendered themselves to the music,
to listening to and enjoying her songs. How those songs
revealed and unfolded her rich and quivering inner
life. . . .

But that other little being kept moving inside her.
And while, forgetting herself, she gave herself up to the
cheerful tempo of the melodies, lavishing her songs in all
directions, deep down in her heart she understood clearly
with the sudden sharpness of a stabbing knife that now,
here on the stage, she was playing the tragic role invented
for drama and opera: to sing and smile regardless of the
pains and fears that break the heart and rend the soul.
. . . Everything—her life, the theater, those women
sitting out there—seemed as unreal to her as if she were
seeing them in a vision or a dream. Only one thing was
real: the pain that choked her throat and made her
breast heave, growing more and more unbearable with
every movement of the child, and as in the old, now
almost forgotten plays, she trembled with the fear of
not being able to hold back her burning tears when
her songs and bearing had to exude joy and happiness.

When the curtain finally fell, she broke down. She

staggered to a sofa, hid her head in her hands, and cried bitterly.

Why? How? Whither?

Nova Misao (Belgrade), January 1, 1954[a]

[a] A condensed version of this article appeared in *Life* Magazine under the title, "A Romance That Rocked Yugoslavia," in the April 12, 1954 issue. This article and various other sources noted that the hero and heroine of the article were, in fact, the then-newlywed Yugoslav Army Chief-of-Staff, General Peko Dapcevic and his bride, Milena Versajkov, whose marriage had taken place early in the summer of 1953. One of the marriage witnesses was Djilas himself, the other Colonel-General Ratko Vujovic, First Army Commander Rear Area (the districts around Belgrade), both friends of the groom. The beautiful lady at the entrance of the stadium was said to be Milica S. Vukmanovic-Tempo, wife of the General, then top Yugoslav economic planner, and now Chairman of the Trade Unions and a Politburo member.

REVOLUTION

At the first reappearance of the old class, the giant, energetic, vital forces of revolution are set in motion as if life and death were at stake. Yugoslav unity, social ownership, and independence have made the revolution a reality. The attack on the spectre of the past is a surging of new life against something which no longer actively exists but is not yet totally dead.

The problem is no longer how to defend or explain the revolution, because it has already become an integral part of society; rather, it is how the revolution should be further developed without being perverted.

Why did our revolution "prefer" disguise? It was victorious without loudly proclaiming its "final goal" or socialism. Until the conflict with Moscow, our revolution was not even called by its real name. It was disguised by the modest terms "national liberation struggle" or "war of national liberation," etc. True, this disguise was not without use. In fact, events thus progressed more easily. Like every other reality, it found itself the nicest, most suitable dress. In the struggle against "socialist" hegemony in 1948, however, this unrealistic disguise was discarded. Why do so many today speak of the revolution and in its behalf, even those whom it did not greatly inspire? Is it still a reality, or is another reality being born within it, which wishes to hide behind its fiery attire?

Of course, as far as the violent struggle for power is concerned, the revolution ended long ago. What is actually taking place now is a revolution in social relations. Society could not continue to progress in the relations and forms which arose during the revolution. Two lines of development are now possible: either transforming the revolutionary (therefore democratic) forms into bureaucratic ones, or transforming these same forms into truly democratic ones. Both are actually taking place. No single form changes easily and "neatly" into another, not even during longer periods of peaceful development. Inevitably, ideological, political, organizational and other kinds of contrasts, difficulties and confusions arise. And so, today, bureaucratism sometimes disguises itself with revolutionary ardor and considers democracy as its successor. To some extent, bureaucracy is at least formally correct, because it insists on the forms of the revolution (concentration of all power in the hands of the Party, and the absence of a written law). Democracy, however, is fundamentally the correct form because it considers the revolution the highest form of democracy in a class society and, therefore, sees itself as the revolution's successor.

During the revolution, the Party united in itself all democratic forces and aspirations. It did so and could do so because it was the representative of the will and action of the masses, and the organized expression of that will and action. Accordingly, the Party was the form of an objective process, a conscious, organized form—and a decisive one because of that organization and consciousness—for further progress. But if it was that then, and had to be so, this does not mean that the Party received a permanent option automatically to remain in the same form during future progress, and so remain the expression of the will and action of the masses. Democracy in the revolution was expressed through the action of the masses, but also through its most conscious nucleus, the revolutionary cadres, and first and foremost, the Party was just that. It is not accidental that Party forums and communists were then not only the focus of the uprising, but also the source of justice, equality, altruism and humanity.[1]

Today, however, relations have changed substantially. This is no longer the same Party which existed during the revolution, at least not for everybody nor in everything. The old revolutionary and democratic spirit is still strong and prevails in the leading cadres, but it is not the only spirit. And this is also roughly true of the Party's structure. Nor can the Party play the same role in the same form as it did during the revolution; it is impossible under the present objective conditions. Its role must now be different and it must take on a different form. Democracy can no longer be achieved by or through armed force. Today, democracy can only be realized peacefully, by developing democratic social relations. During the revolution, the laws were the expression of the will and action of the masses, or the subjective will of the forums and communists, which were almost one and the same thing. The will of the masses at that time was revolution and democracy. Today, however, when we already have democratic laws and a socialist society, weak and underdeveloped perhaps, but nonetheless socialist in city and industry, such subjective decision must necessarily pervert behavior into undemocratic, superficial and arbitrary channels.

Continuing the revolution today means renouncing its obsolete forms for the sake of developing its democratic essence through new forms. As a matter of fact, today revolution is reform, peaceful progress, but progress. Progress is possible today only in democratic forms. Changes in reality and in methods mean that political and cultural progress, and progress of all other conceptual kinds, must take place and has already, indeed, taken place. These changed conceptions will fundamentally influence, and already do influence, reality and social relations, and their progress. Precisely because of those changes, precisely because of the peaceful, reformist character of the actual progress of our revolution, all efforts to "raise" the League of Communists to the level of the prewar or wartime Communist Party are impossible, not so much because it is impossible to raise hundreds of thousands to the level of tens of thousands, but because it is impossible to recreate those revolutionary conditions. If someone today really wants to separate himself from the past and from conservatism, he can do so only by fighting for new and concrete democratic forms. Today it is nonsense to struggle for power in a "revolutionary" form, not only because it is unrealistic, but also because it is counter-revolutionary. When revolutionary—really "revolutionary"— tasks are set down today,[2] this is not only totally unrealistic and of no particular importance, but it is also a return to obsolete forms which under present conditions must hinder progress and serve undemocratic aspirations.

It would be much more useful to think about what

can be done with the League of Communists as it is, and with the development of our certainly poor but real democratic forms, than to stagnate in old forms and to dream of things that used to be—even if those things were great—but which, like everything else, cannot be recreated. Today's revolution is democratic practice, which demands a revolutionary vocation and spirit.

Nothing can diminish the importance of the revolution, nor can anything, up to now, be compared with it and its importance. The revolution's soul can be preserved, however, only in real freedom, because it was carried out by free men, for freedom, and in the name of freedom.

Borba, January 7, 1954

[1] And the majority of these are the old and real communist democratic cadres still.

[2] For example, *Borba* of October 4, 1952: "If the fundamental idea, as stated by Comrade Kardelj at the Second Plenum, is understood to mean that the daily basic work of every communist is political, then it will be a laborious job to transform every member of the League of Communists into a communist conscious of the fact that he belongs to a revolutionary movement, and knowing that his basic task is political activity." However, this is neither Comrade Kardelj's fundamental nor secondary idea, and least of all the way "to make a revolutionary." As far as "laborious work" is concerned, such political activity can only be the most boring vexation.